# A Biblical Path for a Prosperous Society

# A Biblical Path for a Prosperous Society

Brian Baugus

LEXINGTON BOOKS
*Lanham • Boulder • New York • London*

Published by Lexington Books
An imprint of The Rowman & Littlefield Publishing Group, Inc.
4501 Forbes Boulevard, Suite 200, Lanham, Maryland 20706
www.rowman.com

6 Tinworth Street, London SE11 5AL, United Kingdom



British Library Cataloguing in Publication Information Available

**Library of Congress Cataloging-in-Publication Data Available**

ISBN: 978-1-4985-6981-1 (cloth)
ISBN: 978-1-4985-6982-8 (electronic)

God has given to men all that is necessary for them to accomplish their destinies. He has provided a social form as well as a human form. And these social organs of persons are so constituted that they will develop themselves harmoniously in the clean air of liberty. Away, then, with quacks and organizers! Away with their rings, chains, hooks, and pincers! Away with their artificial systems! Away with the whims of governmental administrators, their socialized projects, their centralization, their tariffs, their government schools, their state religions, their free credit, their bank monopolies, their regulations, their restrictions, their equalization by taxation, and their pious moralizations!

And now that the legislators and do-gooders have so futilely inflicted so many systems upon society, may they finally end where they should have begun: May they reject all systems, and try liberty; for liberty is an acknowledgment of faith in God and His works.

—Frédéric Bastiat, *The Law*

*Matthew 6:33*

# Contents

# Acknowledgments

A project like this is never the work of one person, and it is proper to acknowledge the others who, in various ways, supported my efforts or contributed to making it a better product. But I must make clear that while I had much help and I made an effort to be thorough and accurate, any errors or omissions are strictly my own.

This book started life as a graduate paper for a class taught by Dr. Richard Wagner at George Mason University, and I thank Dr. Wagner and GMU for giving me the space to explore the intersection of economics and biblical issues. It was buried for a while, then reemerged as a session paper at the Southern Economics Association annual meetings in 2016. Much thanks to SEA for making room for such sessions and to the Institute for Faith, Work and Economics and Dr. Anne Bradley, who organized this one. I am grateful to her and the entire IFWE team for not only supporting me in this way but for their support of many Christian economists and those in related fields. It was from this conference that Joe Parry from Rowman and Littlefield's Lexington Books approached me about turning the paper into this book. Joe, Bryndee Ryan, and team have been professional and responsive to this first-time author and made this process as smooth as possible.

In addition, I thank Pastor Joe Gwynn for reading an early version of the paper to check my theological applications and Pastor Mike Miller for reading a late version and doing the same. Also, thanks to Professor P.J. Hill for reading an early partial version of the book and making some very useful comments. And Peter Schweizer for encouragement and guidance about how the book writing and publishing process works. Also, I extend my gratitude to an anonymous reviewer who read the entire first draft and made several pages of comments that were very useful.

Others who were encouraging and supportive in their own ways include several of my colleagues at Regent University: Dr. Bill Reddinger, Dr. Pete Fraser, and Dr. Joe Bucci. I am sure I am leaving some out and apologize to anyone who deserves mention but I failed to do so; it just shows how many people play a part.

Finally, I thank my wife, Ildiko, and our family for their encouragement and patience as I spent the time needed working on this. As anyone who has undertaken a special project knows, it will not happen without support and understanding from loved ones, and I have just that. Not only would there be no book, but I would not even be a professor without the support and strong encouragement from my wife to get my doctorate ten years after I thought I was done with formal education. As usual, she was right.

To God Be the Glory.

# Preface

This book explores the political economy model found in the Bible, mostly focused, although not exclusively, on the principles established in the fifth book of the Christian and Hebrew scriptures: Deuteronomy. I attempt to restate old truths that were once widely accepted and show that they are still true and still applicable, especially to the problems in the developing world. This book proposes that all a nation needs to prosper is contained in Deuteronomy. It may seem an odd project, as much has been written on economic development and growth by well-respected and established researchers. Aid workers, non-government organizations, governments of wealthy countries, and large international institutions run and staffed by experts have done much in the field. With all this intellect, training, resources, and political might brought to the problem and decades of experience behind us, what can I possibly offer that is new? And what could the Bible possibly say that is useful on this topic? These are questions I have been asked, and they deserve an answer. Ultimately it is up to the reader to decide the answers and I will state quite willingly up front, I will offer only a little that is new. The Bible has been around a long time, but it is often not applied to political-economic issues in a holistic way. I think a fair reading will lead one to conclude that the Bible has quite a bit to say on this topic worth rediscovering, which may be like a new revelation.

But we are making progress on poverty, so do we need more discussion on this topic? Much progress *has* been made. In the last forty years the number of people living in extreme poverty, frequently although clumsily defined as those living on roughly less than two US dollars a day, both in absolute numbers and as a percentage of world population, has shrunk significantly, even as the total world population has grown. Most of this progress has been realized by small but important economic liberalization steps in China, India, and a few other places such as Brazil and Indonesia. This should be celebrated. It is very good news, although fragile and easily undone either by totalitarian impulses or corruption; as Adam Smith (I want the reader to be fully informed and have included a short biography of every researcher/thinker I reference in Appendix A) wrote in a letter to Sir John Sinclair, "there is a great deal of ruin in a nation."[1] Good trends are not necessarily predictors of the future. According to the World Bank, as recently as the year 2000 about 40 percent, or 1.2 billion of the combined populations of China, India, and Indonesia[2] were in extreme poverty. In 2013 those percentages had fallen to 11.2, 21.2, and 15.9 respectively, and the growth in China alone accounted for 400 million people moving out of extreme poverty, an unbelievably massive improvement in a very short time. But this was easy compared to what is left to do; we should not be lulled into thinking the entire world is moving in the right direction. Global growth has been impressive but very uneven, with many countries growing but very slowly, some going backward or stagnating, and a few seemingly on the brink of economic disaster. Growth is a result of deliberate actions and policies, not inevitable due to the passage of time.

Depending on the estimates used, there are between 700 million and one billion people still living in extreme poverty. Below is a table of the countries in which, according to the World Bank, a majority of the population is living in extreme poverty.

Some other countries probably belong on this list but do not report. Other organizations will give slightly different figures and rankings, but the overall list will be basically the same. And, we should keep in mind, a country with 40 percent of its population in extreme poverty is not on this list but is certainly not an economic success story. This list should be seen as the lower limit, not an exhaustive compilation. As the reader will notice, the overwhelming majority of poor countries are in sub-Sahara Africa; about half of those living in extreme poverty around the globe are in these countries. This is the challenge we face; growth and progress will come not from changes in a few big nations where reforms and changes can be leveraged across many people but in many small, different nations where change has limited impact on the total problem since it stops at the next border. The challenge and goal is to find a way to bring positive reforms and change to as many of these countries as possible. Christians need to understand what their scriptures say about these issues. Many easily see the brokenness in the economic world with poverty, waste, and corruption but do not know what the Bible teaches about economics and can and often do find themselves unknowingly supporting and giving support to policies and systems that caused the very brokenness they think they are addressing.

**Table P.1.1. Nations with Majorities in Extreme Poverty[1]**

| *Country* | *Percent in Extreme Poverty* | *Region* |
|---|---|---|
| Equatorial Guinea | 76.8 | Sub-Saharan Africa |
| Madagascar | 75.3 | Sub-Saharan Africa |
| Zimbabwe | 72.3 | Sub-Saharan Africa |
| Democratic Republic of the Congo | 71.3 | Sub-Saharan Africa |
| Guinea-Bissau | 69.3 | Sub-Saharan Africa |
| Eritrea | 69.0 | Sub-Saharan Africa |
| Burundi | 66.9 | Sub-Saharan Africa |
| Liberia | 63.8 | Sub-Saharan Africa |
| Swaziland | 63.0 | Sub-Saharan Africa |
| Central African Republic | 62.0 | Sub-Saharan Africa |
| São Tomé and Príncipe | 61.7 | Sub-Saharan Africa |
| Honduras | 60.0 | Central America |
| Niger | 59.5 | Sub-Saharan Africa |
| Zambia | 59.3 | Sub-Saharan Africa |
| Togo | 58.7 | Sub-Saharan Africa |
| Haiti | 58.5 | Caribbean |
| Lesotho | 56.6 | Sub-Saharan Africa |
| Guinea | 55.2 | Sub-Saharan Africa |
| Mozambique | 54.7 | Sub-Saharan Africa |
| Guatemala | 53.7 | Central America |
| Sierra Leone | 52.9 | Sub-Saharan Africa |
| Mexico | 51.3 | North America |
| Malawi | 50.7 | Sub-Saharan Africa |
| South Sudan | 50.6 | Sub-Saharan Africa |

1. Max Roser and Esteban Ortiz-Ospina, "Global Extreme Poverty," March 2017, https://ourworldindata.org/extreme-poverty.

This is where I hope this book helps. Eleven of the twenty African countries on the list above are majority Christian and are familiar with the Bible. Another five are Muslim majority, and while their views on the Bible differ from Christians, they still accept it as scriptures.[3] In addition, the most populous country on the list, Mexico, is also majority Christian. It is my hope to explore and explain the economic lessons contained in a document millions of people from all cultures and countries broadly accept as true. The Bible does not belong to any nation or school of thought and is, even in an increasingly secular world, widely respected. I hope to show the lessons that descend from a higher source to address this pressing problem. But that truth is not doing any good if it is not understood. This book seeks to explain what many theologians miss since they have a different focus and what economists miss since the Bible is seldom on our reading list.

I thank you for joining me in this exploration, whether you are a citizen of a developing country, a student, a professional, or just interested in these issues and ideas. I welcome you and hope you find the time you spend in this book worthwhile. I think of this book as a contribution to an ongoing conversation. Ultimately my goal is to serve God by serving others in some small way. If I am able to contribute to the well-being, prosperity, and education of even a few, I will consider this time well spent.

## NOTES

1. Ian Simpson Ross, *The Life of Adam Smith*, 2nd ed. (Oxford: Oxford University Press, 2010), 32.
2. Max Roser and Esteban Ortiz-Ospina, "Global Extreme Poverty," March 2017, https://ourworldindata.org/extreme-poverty.
3. *The CIA World Factbook* (Washington, D.C.: United States Government, n.d.), https://www.cia.gov/library/publications/the-world-factbook/wfbExt/region_afr.html.

# *Part 1*

# WHAT EXACTLY IS THIS BOOK?

## IS THIS A RELIGIOUS BOOK?

The Bible is a spiritual document. Its primary purpose is explaining Christianity and instructing believers in proper faith and practice. Two other faiths, Judaism and Islam, also accept some portion of the Christian scriptures as part of their canon, but I am a Christian economist and this book is written from that perspective, not in any deliberate attempt to exclude anyone else but it is the perspective I have and hold. I believe that all of scripture points to one historical fact, the crucifixion and resurrection of Jesus Christ, and one main article of faith that His punishment was substitutionary for me and is available to anyone else.

That said, this is not a religious book. I do not intend it to be some sort of biblical commentary. That is not my area of expertise. I am examining what may be thought of as one of many secondary purposes, applying biblical principles to a modern practical temporal issue: global poverty and economic growth. These sorts of applications can be believed and applied by those of different faiths or no faith. Much, like the biblical prohibitions on murder and theft, can be believed by all and seen as making society better regardless of one's faith; so too do other principles such as those pertaining to creating a prosperous economy and a flourishing society. Christians may believe what I write because it is in the Bible (and some Christians may disagree with my interpretation as well; I will address that along the way), but non-Christians may believe what I write because it is also supported with research and experience. Truth is truth. And the truth is that most economic development, the massive increase in material well-being over the last 400–500 years, occurred in Christian nations. Yes, there were fits and starts and temporary periods of wealth and growth around the globe and throughout history, but the fact of the matter is, as Deidre McCloskey[1] (see Appendix A) points out in much more detail then I will here, the massive betterment was at first a Dutch and soon after a British phenomenon and spread from there, either by those following or copying them or on their ships of trade and colonization. Rodney Stark (see Appendix A) argues that the era of wealth creation we are still in started further back than McCloskey does, he puts it at the thirteenth century in Italy, and makes a stronger case for its Christian foundation than McCloskey does. Regardless of which view, or some other, you take, the fact is that the huge wealth creation system commonly known, if somewhat improperly, as capitalism, has its roots and development in Western civilization, which, more than any other, is built on biblical principles. However, I want to make a subtle but important distinction here. A people need not be Christian to grow and prosper. It helps since, as I argue, all the necessary ingredients to grow and prosper are contained in the Bible and a Christian people is more likely to encounter those ideas, believe them, and act on them, but truth is truth and it works regardless of who may be using it or what else they may believe. The sun shines on everyone. God established this world and the laws that govern it, both physical and social, none of which can be violated without consequences. We see this clearly in the physical: jump out of a plane and you will fall. We see this less so in the social because it usually takes longer to see effects and the social is much more complex. But it is true just the same. Societies that do not protect property rights or life or do not have a culture of honesty and truthfulness or do not respect human dignity as fiercely as God does, are less prosperous, but there are so many other factors and moving parts that many may not see the connection as clearly as an object falling from a plane.

## THE ETERNAL ECONOMICS QUESTION

Economics basically began with a question about poverty. Adam Smith, the Scottish moral philosopher who did the most to establish economics as a separate academic discipline, began the entire profession by stating as the title of his seminal work, "*[An Inquiry into] The Nature and Causes of the Wealth of Nations*." To a large extent that is the question all economists have wrestled with in some measure. I think we can see how far we have come (or not) by looking at another book title from just a few years ago, this time from Deidre McCloskey's trilogy on economic development history, *Bourgeois Dignity: Why Economics Can't Explain the Modern World.* So, Smith in 1776 wanted to know why some were rich and others were not, and McCloskey, in 2010, is arguing that much of what we have done to try to answer that question has failed. So maybe there is room for some other contributions and, as is often the case in such conundrums, the answers may not need to be discovered but rediscovered.

Space limitations and respect for the reader's time and patience constrain me from detailing all the different theories that have been offered for why some are rich and others are not. There are many theories and much disagreement as to what is vital for economic growth and, by extension, what is the best way to assist the less developed nations. Some argue that poverty is a historical vestige of colonialism and slavery or even further back with geography and animal interaction; others argue it is about legal systems and others about property rights or human rights or ideas and innovation or that it is about more aid and debt relief and on and on. Some of these I discuss and others I leave for your own investigation, but they are all out there competing for time and attention. I am largely pushing all of that discussion to one side to focus on what I think are the main factors I see in the Bible and will deal with modern research and theories if and when it is appropriate to the discussion. I will use the scriptures to cut through some of the intellectual clutter and hopefully get focused on the true core of what allows a people to prosper.

## WHAT DOES THE BIBLE REALLY HAVE TO SAY ABOUT ECONOMICS?

The Bible holds a unique place in Western civilization. It is a foundational document; our understanding of how a civilization should operate comes at least in part from its teachings. Things ranging from the seven-day week to our understanding of charity have biblical origins. However, as with other vital works that are frequently referenced and seldom read, many want to claim the Bible supports their particular view of how society should be ordered. People lay all sorts of interpretations on the Bible including by supposed experts and then others lay interpretation on what the experts have said. My focus is not on delineating what this or that theologian claims and believes. I accept as axiomatic that religious scholarship and opinion, like development theories, are all over the ideological/philosophical map. But there is a distinction between religion, a manmade institution which has been put to the service of all sorts of causes both liberal and tyrannical, and being true to the text. In some circumstances religious institutions and the text are congruent but where they are not, we must remember the text does not change and often the plainest interpretation is the best; think of it as an Occam's Razor of exegesis. In this exploration my focus is on the text and what it says and not the many interpretations theologians and others have claimed for it. Most people do not and have not read the Bible the way I do for this book. I am an economist doing my best to read the Bible carefully but with a specific purpose. I may fall short in places and for that I apologize ahead of time but hope some view those shortcomings as opportunities to join the conversation.

There was a time when scholars and defenders of the liberal[2] order held that the Bible was a reliable and worthy source in support of their cause. It is true that some, like David Hume (see Appendix A), had a visceral reaction to the religious and spiritual but many accepted the Jewish and Christian scriptures, if not as a definitive authority on spiritual matters at least as a worthy contribution to understanding how to form a liberal society. The Bible addresses many issues, people are often surprised to discover how many verses deal with practical everyday life issues; there are hundreds of verses that deal with money management, work habits and employment, marital relations, neighborly relations, crime and punishment, and so forth. The Bible's veracity in such matters was widely accepted before the Enlightenment as we see theologians like the Spanish scholastics and most of the Reformers, secular scholars, political essayists, and creators of entire new orders like the American Founding Fathers reference the Christian tradition and quote Christian scriptures directly in support of their cause. It may be apocryphal but supposedly King George III referred to the American Revolution as a Presbyterian Parson's rebellion but it is the case that the Founding Fathers of the United States relied heavily on the Bible for justification of their constitutional project; the Bible, and specifically the book of Deuteronomy, is the most-quoted source document in the founders' letters, pamphlets et al., more than Hume, Montesquieu, or all the Enlightenment thinkers *combined.*[3]

In the post-Enlightenment age in which we live, references to religious texts have become passé in many circles; such references are seen as a throwback to the Scholastics, mystics, and the Dark Ages along the same lines as alchemy and flat earth theories. It is true that religious institutions and those who ran them have and still do occasionally stand in the way of intellectual progress and have served as agents of oppression for various reasons. This behavior is most often tied to the desire for earthly power and often involves contorted interpretations of scripture when compared to orthodox understanding. There is a reason some religious leaders have not encouraged their followers to read their scriptures; what they are teaching and what the text says frequently differ. But it is also a historical fact that when practice and teaching have differed and the practice has resulted in harm to others and deviated from the text, it has frequently been other Christians calling the abusers out and working toward correction. Reformers and Puritans addressing church abuses and the devout William Wilberforce driving for abolition and Reverend Martin Luther King Jr. leading the cause of racial equality are but a few examples of those motivated by their faith to address wrongs and injustices that were best understood as deviations from true faith. But it is not unique to Christianity to use ideology or philosophy to oppress; there has been much harm done in the name every systemized philosophy and ideology. The point is abuse and misuse is not something that should be laid solely at the feet of Christianity as some are wont to do, it is a human condition.

Abandoning Christian scriptures (or any text) because modern scholars think modern scholarship has transcended their use and value betrays a certain intellectual vanity and risks the loss of valuable insight and understanding. Many modern scholars of all fields are far more concerned with the 'modern prevailing critical trends' than they are in ancient truths that may be contained in ancient writings. This seems especially true in areas with so much scholarly unsettledness, like development economics, which is strongly grounded in history, a large part of our understanding is examining what has worked and what has failed. Many doctoral programs in economics have abandoned teaching a course in history of economic thought. By one measure there are only sixty-three schools in the world with a reputable program in the history of economic thought and only twenty-two in economic history,[4] and even fewer see any value in looking at religious texts in any serious scholarly way. This reflects a change in mainstream economics over the years but also a certain intellectual hubris that is unbecoming of serious scholarly work.

This book examines the text, primarily, but not exclusively, the book of Deuteronomy and attempts to restore it as a valuable source document for those looking to explain, defend, and perpetuate the liberal social order, especially for those studying the origins of the liberal order and operating in the development field. This book is an exploration of the earliest liberal ideas that lay the groundwork for prosperity, or, to blend the economics and biblical language, I ask, and hopefully answer the question, what factors, institutions, and cultural attitudes create a land that flows with milk and honey? That is what this project is about and I am glad you have joined it.

## WHY DEUTERONOMY?

The Bible is a spiritual document with a particular spiritual purpose. However, in accomplishing its spiritual goal it touches on many temporal issues; the majority of the Ten Commandments are about how to get along with other people, for example. Nor is it silent on a proper social order to create prosperity and flourishing. While there are many passages about government and economics throughout the Bible, the book of Deuteronomy, the fifth and final book of Moses, has a unique purpose; it is the most complete and thorough statement in the Bible of what a proper society looks like. God had told His people that He would take them to the Promised Land, which flowed with milk and honey.[5] In other words, the land would be a place of wealth and prosperity *if* the people dedicated themselves to living by God's laws and commands.

This purpose makes Deuteronomy a political document as well as a spiritual one; it is not wrong to say that Deuteronomy is a national constitution. In reality, Deuteronomy has several purposes and there are subsets of laws and commands that are woven together; there are rules and guidelines regarding worship and spiritual matters, there are rules and guidelines on how to keep the nation of Israel pure and holy, and there are rules and guidelines in place to help the Jewish people flourish and prosper as a new nation. The first two categories have application to the faithful. Notions on purity and more narrowly defined acceptable behavior fall into the moral and spiritual purpose of the book and have specific spiritual application. Some of these may appear to be archaic or even barbaric to a modern post-Enlightenment secular person; critics point to passages where stoning and slavery and other behaviors and consequences seem acceptable and we certainly do not want to ignore those. I will address many of them, but perspective is needed. After all, we largely consider the American Constitution a liberal, freedom-enhancing, market-oriented document and it allowed slavery, permitted shameful treatment of the American Indian and disenfranchised women. Such concerns should not disqualify the document from having value and usefulness and within context may be seen in a different light. I do not want to shrug off the controversial parts of the book, too many Christian teachers ignore these hard verses and many critics focus only on them. I deal with them thoroughly, but proper scholarship demands that I approach it with the same consistency as any other document, interpreted by the entirety of the document and set in its historical context.

In short, Deuteronomy is, at least in part, a political-economic document, and as such is the only political-economic document in the Bible and is one of the oldest such documents in existence. There are significant passages in the Bible that deal with political and economic issues and I look at some, but Deuteronomy has special place as the constitution for the fledging nation of Israel. Proof of this claim comes from many places. The document itself states that it is a political constitution with a purpose. In chapter 4 we read: "And now, O Israel, listen to the statutes and the rules that I am teaching you, and do them, that you may live, and go in and take possession of the land that the Lord, the God of your fathers, is giving you."[6]

So, it is the statutes and rules by which Israel must live, and then chapter 6 tells them why they should follow these statutes and rules:

> Now this is the commandment—the statutes and the rules—that the Lord your God commanded me to teach you, that you may do them in the land to which you are going over, to possess it, that you may fear the Lord your God, you and your son and your son's son, by keeping all his statutes and his commandments, which I command you, all the days of your life, and that your days may be long. Hear therefore, O Israel, and be careful to do them, that it may go well with you, and that you may multiply greatly, as the Lord, the God of your fathers, has promised you, in a land flowing with milk and honey.[7]

It is clear that the purpose is to provide the rules and laws so that the people will live long, prosperous lives.[8] The preamble to the American Constitution has a similar stated purpose, "to secure the Blessings of Liberty to Ourselves and our Posterity . . ."[9]

In addition to the document stating that its purpose is to secure prosperity for generations, we can also look at its form and format and see that it is consistent with other political documents from the region and time period. Deuteronomy is a treaty between God and His people who were most recently a group of former slaves camping in the desert; they were not organized into a nation state and had little notion of how a nation properly functions. They needed instructions on how to get a new nation founded, operational, and headed in the right direction. Deuteronomy provided those instructions in a particular kind of constitutional form common in the ancient Middle East called a Suzerain treaty.

Now, I need to take a small side turn and address an issue I am minimally qualified to address, so I will keep this short, the scholarship on Deuteronomy. Traditional Christian and Jewish scholarship hold that Deuteronomy was written by Moses and possibly the ending by Joshua in the fifteenth century B.C.E. before the Israelites began their conquest of and settlement in Canaan. Since the early nineteenth century and the work of German theologian Wilhelm Martin Leberecht de Wette, many scholars have concluded that Deuteronomy was written in the seventh century B.C.E. by rabbis and scribes in a post-exile Jerusalem as a sort of patriotic document to rally and unite the Jewish people after living in exile. I am not here to address this issue, I have my opinion, but it is for the theologians, archeologists, and historians to debate, not economists. The interesting fact is that regardless of their conclusion on the dating and authorship, the purposes and applications of the book are the same. Deuteronomy was either written for a people emerging from four hundred years of slavery and forty years as little more than a collection of nomadic tribes to instruct them on how to form a prosperous nation serving the true God or it is written to unite and guide a people emerging from captivity and rule by a foreign power (Babylon) and needing help in reestablishing their nation, government, and economy after wars, corruption, and exile. The spiritual implications of this debate are very significant, I am not trying to minimize them, but for our purposes the timing does not make much difference. Deuteronomy had very similar purposes regardless of which theory one holds, but for writing purposes I will assume the traditional dating and authorship when necessary.

That side trip into biblical archeology behind us, we can focus on the issue. Deuteronomy is written in the same formal style as a Suzerain treaty, although it has a significant distinction. Suzerain treaties were common among the Hittites, Assyrians, Egyptians, and other nations in the ancient Middle and Near East. Archeologists have found about fifty such treaties and they are known to have been common political documents[10] usually made between a conqueror or protector and a vassal state. This is where Deuteronomy differs with the traditional Suzerain treaty, while Deuteronomy follows the same pattern as these, with God being the protector and Israel being the vassal, there are several places where the people's assent is recorded. The terms were read aloud and the people affirmed their agreement. This was not a treaty between two kings which was then imposed on the people; the people were actively involved in agreeing to the terms. In this sense it was more of a social contract or maybe more accurately a social covenant than a traditional Suzerain treaty. That said, and I will return to this people's agreement point later, the book does follow the treaty form and these treaties had a definite form and required content as described in Table 1.1.1.

The document (or an ancillary document) would also stipulate where the treaty was to be stored, could detail the blessings and curses for obedience or lack thereof, and often include a required public reading of the document on a regular basis. In sum, Deuteronomy is a document designed to establish a political-economic system that would enable a people who had been oppressed and disunited for centuries to create a prosperous and flourishing society. In that sense, the world has several dozen nations that are in a similar history and these ideas are just as applicable now as then.

## WHAT IS ECONOMIC GROWTH?

Since this book's goal is to show how Deuteronomy lays out the framework for a prosperous and growing society, it only makes sense to define our terms at the outset. The standard economic measure for growth is Gross Domestic Product, a monetary measure of all goods produced and purchased within a

**Table 1.1.1. The Basic Form of an Ancient Suzerain Treaty**[1]

| *Item* | *Purpose* | *Relevant Passages in Deuteronomy*[2] |
|---|---|---|
| Preamble | Names the parties involved in the treaty often identifying them by genealogy and title | 1:1–5 |
| Prologue | Details deeds performed by the Suzerain for the vassal and history of relationship up to that point and vassal agrees to continue this relationship | 1:6–4:29 |
| Stipulations | Explains the duties, expectations, and responsibilities of both parties. May also detail the blessing for obedience and punishments for disobedience | Chapters 5–26 |
| Ratification | Where both parties publicly agree, often calling on their deities to serve as witness, to the treaty, in most cases this was done between kings or their representatives but in Israel's case in involved all the people | Chapters 27–34—includes curses and blessings for obedience |

1. Hill and Walton, *A Survey of the Old Testament*, 142–43.
2. Meredith G. Kline, *Treaty of the Great King: The Covenant Structure of Deuteronomy* (Eugene, OR: Wipf & Stock Publishers, 1963).

nation's borders in a given period of time. I find this measure, as do many of my colleagues, unsatisfying. It has value and uses but is overused; like any tool it has its purpose but is not well suited for many other uses and can actually cause harm, like trying to hammer a screw into a window frame. GDP gives a big-picture overview but can be very misleading, even in developed countries. It is primarily a measure of spending and spending at the national level correlates with, but does not equate to, improvement in the average person's life. This disconnect is demonstrated by just one sad episode from relatively recent history when in 1976 President Bokassa of the Central African Republic spent 20 percent of its GNP (the older similar measure to GDP) crowning himself emperor.[11] Lots of spending but a big waste and no improvement for the people. But to GDP all spending looks the same.

We need to focus on how the average person is doing. This is tricky even with modern data collection methods and statistical analysis and often involves qualitative data as well as quantitative, especially in nations in which data collection is poor and significant portions of economic activity are not recorded. GDP does not capture many forms of valuable economic activity so, while I will refer to GDP from time to time, I am far more interested in various (sometimes creative) ways to assess how a nation's people are doing.

As you read this book I will present measures on corruption, literacy rates, inefficiencies and waste, and other creative ways to assess what can improve the average person's life even if GDP does not reflect it.

A final thought before the next chapter starts the heart of the book. I do not claim this is a thorough and comprehensive treatise. This is designed to be an accessible survey of the forgotten and overlooked political-economic truths contained in the Bible. If the reader finds him or herself saying "what about this?" then I will reply ahead of time "you are probably correct." This book could be twice as long and much more detailed but, I remind you, this is a contribution to an ongoing conversation that will and should continue, maybe by you.

## NOTES

1. See McCloskey's *Bourgeois Trilogy* for her exploration into some of these same issues.

2. A note on usage of the term *liberal*. In modern usage the definition of *liberal* can vary by location and mean the exact opposite of how it is used in other places. I use it here in the historical sense that much of human effort to flourish is involved liberating people from restrictions and constraints, frequently imposed by government, sometimes by the church and others. A liberal society is one that maximizes the freedom of the individual, which necessarily means limiting the power of others, especially government.

3. Donald Lutz, "From Covenant to Constitution in American Political Thought," 1979.

4. Christian Roessler, "Rankings: Economics History & Thought," n.d.

5. R. C. Sproul and Keith A. Mathison, eds., *The Reformation Study Bible: English Standard Version, Containing the Old and New Testaments* (Orlando, Fla. : Phillipsburg, N.J: Ligonier Ministries; Produced and distributed by Presbyterian and Reformed Pub. Co, 2005), Exodus 3:8, Exodus 33:3, and Deuteronomy 6:3. (All biblical references in this book will come from this version of the Bible, henceforth noted as ESV.)

6. Deuteronomy, n.d., 4:1 (ESV).

7. Ibid., 6:1–3 (ESV).

8. It is interesting to note that the Vulcan catchphrase "live long and prosper" and the V-shaped hand signature made popular by Leonard Nimoy's character Mr. Spock from the television and movie franchise *Star Trek* is an ancient Jewish blessing possibly derived from these very verses.

9. "The Constitution of the United States," n.d., Preamble.

10. Andrew Hill and John Walton, *A Survey of the Old Testament* (Grand Rapids, MI: Zondervan Publishing House, n.d.), 142–43.

11. George Ayittey, "Economic Atrophy in Black Africa," *Cato Journal* 7, no. 1 (n.d.): 202.

# *Part 2*

# *Chapter One*

# The Biblical Political Economy Model

## WHY IS THIS BOOK NEEDED?[1]

Because of its spiritual focus, people may be surprised to find how much Deuteronomy emphasizes material prosperity. Deuteronomy talks of making Israel a great nation,[2] for people to have a long and prosperous life,[3, 4] and that Israel should prosper.[5] This is not its main goal and there should not be any confusion that this is about making everyone rich. This is about the biblical system that allows people to pursue their God-given abilities, goals, and skills. This is about how a nation can flourish by structuring itself to follow God's principles; that following the political-economic system laid out in Deuteronomy is a moral and God-pleasing system that results in prosperity and longevity.

There is room for discussion on this topic, modern economics does not fully understand what causes economic growth, many very good and respected scholars disagree and make compelling cases for their respective theory. For the purposes of this paper I am agnostic on the issue of the primary causes of growth, and while we may dispute what is most vital, we can agree that many factors play a role in growth. Indeed, it may be best argued that growth is not due to any one issue but a holistic system in which several factors must all be present for growth to occur; property rights are important but high tax environment with good property rights will not grow much, protecting life is vital but if the courts are crooked in civil and business matters there will be little growth. While modern economists frequently have a research approach of trying to isolate *the* variable in any phenomena they are studying, the world is complex; it may be that no one variable is the answer, that the key variables are not easily captured in a quantitative way, and/or there is high degree of interdependence between the variables. The point is, there is no *one* key. This is not a new thought but as one critic recently put it, modern research is devoted to finding statistical significance and much of the world does not work that way. Few today think in holistic systems like Smith and Marx.

Deuteronomy is a holistic political-economic document that establishes an entire system. It states as much in several places, that all the commandments must be followed if the people want to prosper. We see this concept stated at the very beginning of the book, after some historical context in chapters 1–3 the book begins in earnest in chapter 4 with this: "And now, O Israel, listen to the statutes and the rules that I am teaching you, and do them, that you may live, and go in and take possession of the land that the LORD, the God of your fathers, is giving you."[6] And, later in the same chapter, Moses states, "Therefore you shall keep his statutes and his commandments, which I command you today, that it may go well with you and with your children after you, and that you may prolong your days in the land that the LORD your God is giving you for all time."[7] And in chapter 6 it states, "Now this is the commandment—the statutes and the rules—that the LORD your God commanded me to teach you, that you may do them in the land to which you are going over, to possess it, that you may fear the LORD your God, you and your son and your son's son, by keeping all his statutes and his commandments, which I command you, all the days of your life, and that your days may be long. Hear therefore, O Israel, and be careful to do them, that it may go well with you, and that you may multiply greatly, as the LORD, the God of your fathers, has promised you, in a land flowing with milk and honey."[8] These are not the only places where following all the commandments is tied to prosperity, the book is very clear about this idea and repeats it frequently, conveying the concept that these are not a menu of choices from which a people can pick and choose but an entire interdependent system.

What follows in the balance of this book is an organizational structure I have imposed on the text for my purposes, which is to show the Deuteronomy path to prosperity, but my goal is always to remain faithful to the text meaning and intent, and so long passages are frequently used to keep the context and sometimes passages will be repeated as support for each other in understanding and meaning.

## NOTES

1. Throughout this paper the reader will be spared the tedious hedging phraseology such as "allegedly" or "supposedly," etc. when referencing something that is attributed to God. The author recognizes that there are a wide range of views regarding the Bible but in an effort to save time and space such terminology is omitted. If the

reader feels the need, please feel free to think the preferred phrases to yourself as you go along.

2. *Deuteronomy*, n.d., 4:6 (ESV).

3. Ibid., 5:33 (ESV).

4. According to Leonard Nimoy, the actor who portrayed the iconic character Mr. Spock in the original television and movie franchise *Star Trek*, the Vulcan blessing "live long and prosper" was taken from a Jewish blessing most likely based on these verses.

5. Ibid., 6:3; 7:13; 8:7–10 (ESV).

6. *Deuteronomy*, 4:1 (ESV).

7. Ibid., 4:40 (ESV).

8. Ibid., 6:1–3 (ESV).

## *Chapter Two*

# Created in the Image of God

## *Human Rights and Dignity*

Deuteronomy covers many human rights issues, prohibiting murder and violence, which I spend more time on in the next chapter, is the minimal standard, as Jesus would explain in the Sermon on the Mount: "You have heard that it was said to those of old, 'You shall not murder; and whoever murders will be liable to judgment.' But I say to you that everyone who is angry with his brother will be liable to judgment; whoever insults his brother will be liable to the council; and whoever says, 'You fool!' will be liable to the hell of fire."[1] This is obvious far more comprehensive than murder and Jesus was just summarizing what Deuteronomy already taught.

Possibly the best measure of how a society respects human rights is how it protects and includes those who are frequently on society's margins or are outright outcasts. Any society that disregards whole classes of citizens and their contribution and creative input is throwing away a valuable resource, not to mention the moral implications.

For all of human history and in many societies up to this very day, certain classes of people have been disregarded and frequently relegated to second-class status or worse. Sometimes this treatment was cultural and traditional but many times it was codified as part of the society's legal framework. In a sense this treatment denied the full personhood of the members of these targeted groups, whether it be gender-based, national origin-based, or class and occupation-based, these supposedly lesser groups were oppressed in various ways. The irony is that such treatment denied and denies society much production and many contributions.

However, Deuteronomy does things differently. Built on the theological concept established early in Genesis, that humans are created in God's image, *imago dei* is the classic theological term, and that simple fact alone makes each individual, regardless of any other characteristics, worthy of respect, dignity, and full personhood. That does not mean all have the same roles or will be or should be equal in outcomes but all are worthy of respect and certain rights and considerations. Deuteronomy and a few other passages explain what that looks like in daily society.

## WOMEN

Historically and in some places today women are viewed as second-class citizens, and in many cases were viewed as property and even expendable. Deuteronomy has a different approach. Physical violence against a woman's person is always a first concern and I deal with that in the next chapter. However, for women in that time period, or even this one, physical violence may not have been as much of a concern as other considerations such as being destitute and forgotten and basically cast aside. We can see this in the fact that Deuteronomy takes special care to address how women in different places of life are to be treated and preserves their dignity and worth.

### Widows

Widows have long been viewed as highly expendable by many societies. Some North American tribes expected older widows to go and die, once their purpose of tending to a family and helping a husband was done, they were considered a tribal burden to be eliminated. But one need not go back in time to see such behavior; in several places today widows are outcasts such as in parts of India. The city of Vrindavan, one hundred miles south of Dehli, is known as the "city of widows" because of the large concentration of women who are no longer wanted by their families living there. "Even relatives who don't literally drive a widow from the family home can make it plain every day that her role among them has ended—that a widow in India, forever burdened by the misfortune of having outlived her husband, is physically alive but socially dead," in the words of Delhi psychologist Vasantha Patri, who has written about the plight of India's widows. So, because Vrindavan is known as a "city of widows," a possible source of hot meals and companionship and purpose, they also come alone, on buses or trains, as they have for generations. "None of us wants to go back to our families," a spidery woman named Kanaklata Adhikari declared in firm Bengali from her bed in the shelter room she shares with seven other widows. "We never talk to our families. We are our family."[2]

The Britain-based Loomba Foundation is very active in securing basic rights for widows around the world and chronicles many stories like the one above. Whether it is cultural tradition or formal and legally enforced, the fact is that in many countries, widows are seen as a burden. Deuteronomy is different. Women were accorded full-citizen status in Deuteronomy and widows were specifically singled out for special care and attention: "For the Lord your God is God of gods and Lord of lords, the great, the mighty, and the awesome God, who is not partial and takes no bribe. He executes justice for the fatherless and the widow, and loves the sojourner, giving him food and clothing."[3] I will return to orphans and immigrants but for now, we see that Deuteronomy warns the people not only to not kill widows (seems like the minimal responsibility to most reading this but only because the Bible has taught us such, as we can see the natural inclination is to rid society of widows), but that God will defend them and ensure they get justice and therefore all the people should treat them justly.

Later, God equates the widow to the priest and ties Israel's future prosperity to how the people treat widows, among others:

> When you have finished paying all the tithe of your produce in the third year, which is the year of tithing, giving it to the Levite, the sojourner, the fatherless, and the widow, so that they may eat within your towns and be filled, then you shall say before the Lord your God, 'I have removed the sacred portion out of my house, and moreover, I have given it to the Levite, the sojourner, the fatherless, and the widow, according to all your commandment that you have commanded me. I have not transgressed any of your commandments, nor have I forgotten them. I have not eaten of the tithe while I was mourning, or removed any of it while I was unclean, or offered any of it to the dead. I have obeyed the voice of the Lord my God. I have done according to all that you have commanded me. Look down from your holy habitation, from heaven, and bless your people Israel and the ground that you have given us, as you swore to our fathers, a land flowing with milk and honey.'[4]

Not only were widows not to be starved or run off but they were, by special decree, to be fed and taken care of as an act that was pleasing to God. This is a theme that carries through the entire Christian Bible as there are over seventy verses in both testaments commanding God's people to take care of widows and treat them well.

## Divorce

Another situation where women were at great risk was when they were divorced. Divorce has had a stigma in the West that only relatively recently, for better or for worse, has started to diminish. But even if the stigma is mostly gone, the consequences, which are largely negative, still prevail. There are two sets of consequences of divorce; one impact is to the people involved and those consequences impact women disproportionately. The second is, if divorce becomes widespread and commonly accepted it may well have negative impacts on the larger society with broken homes and children in confusion about family life and, in some, creating psychological issues that last long into adulthood. I will focus on the micro effects to the family, and on the woman in particular, in this section, but we need to understand that events that happen at the family and local levels will ultimately have larger impact.

Divorce is a horrible thing in God's eyes. "For the man who does not love his wife but divorces her, says the LORD, the God of Israel, covers his garment with violence, says the LORD of hosts. So guard yourselves in your spirit, and do not be faithless."[5] In another translation it reads God hates divorce. Divorce frequently left the woman in a very vulnerable situation, her security and protection and old age care system were gone, she was less attractive in the marriage market, and destitution was possible. As another translation puts it, the man "does violence to the one he should protect, says the LORD Almighty."[6] The notion that the husband should protect the wife may strike some modern ears as old-fashioned, out-of-date, or even chauvinistic. But the hard facts are that divorce impacted women much more than men, it could truly be a matter of life and death for the woman.

However, these consequences should not be viewed as exclusively an ancient problem. A paper by Stephen Jenkins of the Britain-based Institute for Social and Economic Research reports that not much has changed:

> In the past two decades, as panel surveys have become widespread, substantial evidence has accumulated concerning the economic consequences of marital disruption measured in terms of the change in some measure of net household income adjusted for differences in household size and composition. Almost without exception, these studies have found large falls in income in the year after a marital split for separating women. National studies covering Britain, Canada, and the USA include Bianchi and McArthur (1989), Bianchi et al. (1999), David and Flory (1989), Duncan and Hoffman (1985), Finnie (1993), Hoffman (1977), Jarvis and Jenkins (1998, 1999), McKeever and Wolfinger (2001), and Smock (1993, 1994).[7]

Jenkins also finds that:

> The patterns of income changes between men, women and children correspond closely to those found in earlier studies, and Jarvis and Jenkins (1999), in particular. Separating wives and children fare much worse than separating husbands. According to the 'all waves' estimates, the median income change for separating wives is –22 per cent, for separating husbands +13 per cent, and for children –19 per cent. For separating wives, there is little difference in the

> median change according to whether there were dependent children present at the pre-split interview: –21 per cent for those without children, and –23 per cent for those with children.[8]

The U.S. Census shows the same sort of post-divorce income disparity. In 2015 married households had a median income of $84,626 while households headed by women had a median income of $37,797. These are not single, never married women, that is a separate category, but households headed by a woman with other members living in the house. While this category contains several sub-categories, the majority belong to one of two groups: never married mothers and divorced mothers. For the purposes of this discussion these two groups are essentially identical. By comparison, single females who are not mothers have a median annual income of a little over $29,000.

Male-headed households, fathers with no wife/mother in the home, had a median income of 55,861. This is 70 percent greater than similarly situated women. Single males have a median annual income of a little over $40,000.

Making some basic, but not heroic assumptions, we can see how bad an economic deal divorce is for women. It is not good for men either in some ways, but it is disproportionately bad for women. For example, if we take a married couple earning the median $84,262 and assume that, regardless of the source of income each partner has a claim on half of it, then each spouse has $42,131 at his or her disposal. If they divorce, then her income falls 10 percent while his increases 32.5 percent. In addition, it is likely that she will have the larger responsibility for the children, even if the father pays adequate child support to help equalize the income gap there is a high opportunity cost in the time spent being the custodial parent. Table 2.2.1 below is a partial reproduction from the census report and presents the basic income figures.

This data is for the United States. The income differences are only proportionally more exaggerated in lower income nations and sometimes still life and death hang in the balance for the woman as it was in the ancient world.

It may be tempting to analyze these data and conclude that a divorced man's income increases to $55,861 and a divorced woman's is $37,797, for a total of $93,658, which is greater than the $84,626 they made when married. But this analysis only looks at the income side of the equation. Beyond the emotional and spiritual aspects, marriage is a coordination move that allows two people to complement schedules, consolidate expenses, and supplement incomes. Divorce is a significant disruption that breaks all those relationships and so that extra $9,000 in combined income has to support two households and all that goes with that, just housing expenses alone will take most of the extra $9,000 so even some sort income redistribution scheme will not make divorce a net economic gain for the couple.

**Table 2.2.1. Income and Earnings Summary Measures by Selected Characteristics: 2014 and 2015**[1]

| Characteristic | 2015 Number (thousands) | 2015 Median income (dollars) Estimate | 2015 Median income (dollars) Margin of error[1] (±) |
|---|---|---|---|
| *HOUSEHOLDS* | | | |
| All households | 125,819 | 56,516 | 528 |
| *Type of Household* | | | |
| Family households | 82,184 | 72,165 | 608 |
| Married-couple | 60,251 | 84,626 | 983 |
| Female householder, no husband present | 15,622 | 37,797 | 995 |
| Male householder, no wife present | 6,310 | 55,861 | 1,595 |
| Nonfamily households | 43,635 | 33,805 | 776 |
| Female householder | 23,093 | 29,022 | 822 |
| Male householder | 20,542 | 40,762 | 745 |

1. https://www.census.gov/library/publications/2016/demo/p60-256.html Table 1 6/26/17

Table 2.2.1 above presents a best-case scenario. In nations where women bear a higher burden of household work either due to stronger adherence to traditional spousal roles or less education, the prospects for a divorced woman are much less promising than even these somewhat dismal statistics show. The fact is women are more harmed by divorce to this very day even in the richest countries where legal status is secure and economic opportunities plentiful. Deuteronomy recognizes this reality even before it was a reality and put in place a process that protects the woman as best it can, given the situation as a whole is unfortunate and has no real positive outcome.

The divorce had to be in writing.[9] The husband was required to present the wife he was divorcing a written document of the divorce which was proof of her freedom to remarry.[10] She was not necessarily resigned to spend the rest of her years alone facing destitution, she had agency to act as a free woman. The requirement to have the divorce in writing has at least two significant implications to consider. One implication is that women had independent standing in court; if there was a dispute over the divorce or the document, she could go to court on her own to resolve it since she possessed a legal document. We see evidence of this in Jesus' parable in Luke 18 about the widow who petitioned a judge on her own. The second implication is that the requirement that the divorce be written implies that women could read. I address female education in the next section, but female literacy is a significant advancement even today in many countries.

There is an alternate explanation to be considered; that most in Israel were illiterate. If this were the case then that made obtaining a written document time-consuming and expensive and therefore very difficult, if not prohibitive, to get a divorce. Scholars are divided on this issue.[11] Text evidence suggests literacy; the scriptures are written, there are commands to teach every child the scriptures (Deuteronomy 6), and there are other legal and written document requirements in the Bible such as property deeds and financial transactions. But either scenario implies a more favorable treatment of women and creates a significant burden on the husband, making the choice to divorce a very serious one not to be undertaken lightly. This burden, combined with the cost and requirements to obtain a bride, made marriage and family very serious business, to be undertaken with soberness and clarity.

Much of the focus on divorce in the Bible is on the men, he must give her a written divorce, he commits violence when he divorces, and so forth. There are a number of admonitions in the Bible directed toward men who should stay with their wives and in their old age love the wife *of* their youth, not a wife *in* her youth, the idea of older successful men attracting younger, pretty wives is not a new one. This might lead some critics to argue the man had all the power, the wife was stuck unless he divorced her, but maybe not. In a teaching on divorce in Mark 10:2–9, Jesus makes an interesting statement:

> And Pharisees came up and in order to test him asked, "Is it lawful for a man to divorce his wife?" He answered them, "What did Moses command you?" They said, "Moses allowed a man to write a certificate of divorce and to send her away." And Jesus said to them, "Because of your hardness of heart he wrote you this commandment. But from the beginning of creation, 'God made them male and female.' Therefore a man shall leave his father and mother and hold fast to his wife, and the two shall become one flesh.' So they are no longer two but one flesh. What therefore God has joined together, let not man separate."[12]

And in the house the disciples asked him again about this matter. And he said to them, "Whoever divorces his wife and marries another commits adultery against her, and if she divorces her husband and marries another, she commits adultery."[13]

Again, most of the focus is on men, their evil, their responsibility or abandonment of it, and the theology of marriage, but the last line of this discourse is particularly insightful for this discussion. Apparently, the wife, at least by Jesus' time, could initiate a divorce as well, and she was held to the same moral standard on the issue as the man was.

Divorce is a bad situation for all involved, from a biblical point of view it is permissible but only preferred under some vary narrow circumstances such as abuse and infidelity. But, in the final analysis, it is almost always worse for the woman and always has been, and Deuteronomy took a number of measures to protect her dignity and future even under the toughest of circumstances.

## Female Education and Empowerment

There is more evidence of the value Deuteronomy places on women; after all, girls being allowed to survive to adulthood is a biological imperative for the species and treating divorce (and marriage) as significant actions not to be taken lightly could just be part of a broader culture of civility and responsibility. Both are important and are significant improvements over many nations of that time or many today, but neither may be uniquely aimed at treating women as full persons valued for just existing. We need to look deeper and in other areas, after all women could still be treated very poorly in their daily lives, surviving childhood and maintaining a relationship puts them on par with a wanted pet or useful farm animal. There is much more to being a fully recognized person with dignity and worthy of respect, and Deuteronomy sees to that.

Women and girls and how they are treated both culturally and in law are significant indicators of how far human rights and the respect for human dignity extends in a society. Rights are not about how the rich, powerful, and elite treat themselves but about how the marginalized are treated and respected. In my class, I tell students to measure a nation's progress not by GDP growth or the GINI index, although those things are useful, but look to women's education attainment and literacy rates and female school attendance statistics. If girls and boys attend school at roughly the same rates and male and female literacy rates are roughly the same then that tells us one important thing; that human rights and dignity extends deeper into society and that means the society has taken a vital step beyond basic rights and in the direction of female equality and ultimately higher economic prosperity. We can see this today and it is true now and it was true then.

According to UNESCO, 86 percent of the world is literate and the gap between the genders is 7.3 percent favoring males so that 90 percent or men are literate and 82.7 percent of women are. This is a remarkable achievement when we think that for most of human history many if not most people were at least functionally illiterate. There are some caveats with the UNESCO statistics; there is no defining standard as what "literate" means, countries are self-reporting and that leads to all sorts of biases and suspicions such as North Korea being the only country reporting a 100 percent literacy rate, and several advanced countries like Switzerland, Japan, France, and the United States not reporting at all. We must think of the statistics as the best-case scenario and questionable in some cases, but it is what we have. Even so, we can see in Table 2.2.2 below, impoverished economies and limited literacy appear to be correlated even if the data is a little too suspect to run any significant test.

**Table 2.2.2. Poverty and Female Literacy**

| *Country* | *Percent in Extreme Poverty*[1] | *Female Literacy Rate*[2] | *Literacy Rate Gender Gap*[3] |
|---|---|---|---|
| Equatorial Guinea | 76.8% | 93.4% | 4.4% |
| Madagascar | 75.3% | 62.6% | 4.1% |
| Zimbabwe | 72.3% | 84.6% | 4.4% |
| Democratic Republic of the Congo | 71.3% | 66.0% | 22.8% |
| Guinea-Bissau | 69.3% | 48.3% | 23.5% |
| Eritrea | 69.0% | 65.5% | 16.9% |
| Burundi | 66.9% | 83.1% | 5.1% |
| Liberia | 63.8% | 32.8% | 29.6% |
| Swaziland | 63.0% | 87.5% | –.1% |
| Central African Republic | 62.0% | 24.4% | 26.4% |
| Average | | 64.8% | 13.7% |

*Note: Female literacy rate refers to adult women between the ages of 15 and 24.*

1. "Poverty & Equity Data Portal" (The World Bank, n.d.),
2. UNESCO Institute for Statistics, "Literacy Rate, Youth Female (% of Females Ages 15–24)" (The World Bank, n.d.), https://data.worldbank.org/.
3. Ibid.

While there are some bright spot exceptions, the ten poorest countries from the table presented earlier in the book have a female literacy rate under 65 percent and, on average, a 13.7 percent gender literacy gap favoring males. Reversing the approach, the ten countries with the largest gender gap are all poor as Table 2.2.3 shows:

**Table 2.2.3. Poverty and Female Literacy Rates**

| *Country* | *Female Literacy Rate*[1] | *Gender Literacy Gap*[2] | *World Poverty Rank*[3] |
|---|---|---|---|
| Yemen | 55.0% | 30.1% | 28 |
| Liberia | 32.8% | 29.6% | 4 |
| Mozambique | 45.4% | 27.9% | 7 |
| Afghanistan | 24.2% | 27.8% | 20 |
| Pakistan | 42.7% | 26.9% | 49 |
| Central African Republic | 24.4% | 26.4% | 1 |
| Senegal | 43.8% | 24.6% | 29 |
| Guinea-Bissau | 48.3% | 23.5% | 13 |
| Togo | 55.3% | 23.0% | 11 |
| Democratic Republic of the Congo | 66.0% | 22.8% | 3 |
| Average | 43.7% | 26.3% | 16.5 |

*Note: Female literacy rate refers to adult women between the ages of 15 and 24.*

1. UNESCO Institute for Statistics, "Literacy Rate, Youth Female (% of Females Ages 15–24)" (The World Bank, n.d.), https://data.worldbank.org/.
2. Ibid.
3. "GDP Per Capita, PPP (Currrent International $)" (The World Bank, n.d.), https://data.worldbank.org/indicator/NY.GDP.PCAP.PP.CD?view=chart,.

## Literacy Then Growth, or Growth Then Literacy?

The natural research question is which comes first: female literacy or economic growth? The theoretical case can be made either way. One could argue that as countries get wealthier, families can afford to go without the work services of children and can afford to send them to school or take time to teach them. This is what we have tended to see in history, only the privileged classes (royalty and wealthy) provided much education to children and even then, girls were second consideration behind the presumed male heir. As the economy grew, then education opportunities expanded.

However, there is another way to look at this. It could be argued that a people can grow faster by educating as many as possible from the start. Resources are limited and choices must be made, but since I am focusing on the biblical model, that is what needs to be analyzed and it is different from the historical experience. Since the command to teach your children was given before Israel entered the Promised Land, the biblical model implies that education comes first and *then* growth. The land will flow with milk and honey, but parents, teach your children right away. After all, how else could they learn and follow scriptures and laws and so forth if they could not read? While the historical experience is a residual model, parents get children an education only after the family has reached a certain level of wealth and productivity, the biblical model is an investment model; teach everyone from the beginning and they will be more productive from the start, and perpetuating that education to future generations will be much less expensive. Making sure all of the population is educated at least at some basic level, literacy and numeracy are the most important skills, instead of only educating a few elites intensely, is the biblical model.

So, what actually happened in Israel? As mentioned earlier, there is scholarly debate on how broad literacy was but there is persuasive evidence to support that literacy was more widespread than one might assume at first glance. In addition to the text evidence mentioned above, later episodes in Jewish history seem to support widespread female literacy, the virtuous woman being described in Proverbs 31 as one who engages in all sorts of business in the marketplace would indicate that girls and women were to be taught to at least read at some level and probably a good bit more including numeracy and other life skills outside of homemaking. Archeological evidence indicates that literacy rates were pretty high by 600 B.C.E.[14] This is about eight hundred years after the traditional dating of Deuteronomy but that literacy had penetrated well beyond the elites is clear. Robson (2007) argues that literacy and numeracy was widespread in Mesopotamia:

> Neolithic villagers used simple geometric counters in clay and stone to record exchange transactions, funded by agricultural surpluses. As societies and economies grew in size and complexity, increasing strain was placed on trust and

> memory, driving both an increasing numerical sophistication and the invention of written signs for the commodities, agents, and actions involved in managing them in the late fourth millennium BC . . . this numerate, literate urbanism in turn pushed both literary and mathematical development, giving rise to the world's first supra-utilitarian mathematics and literature in the territorial kingdoms of southern Iraq over 4,000 years ago.[15]

Ancient Israel is, of course, not Mesopotamia referenced in the research above, but the Semitic founding father Abraham was from that region and the biblical evidence implies that he and his immediate descendants engaged in a number of business transactions, which would have required some basic literacy and numeracy skills.

The point here is not to engage in the archeological debates, we may never truly know, but to present credible evidence that literacy, even female literacy, was possibly widespread, was not prevented or resisted, and seemed encouraged. Female literacy and empowerment are significant indicators of growth and development. As we saw above, poor countries do not educate their girls. Historically, this has been somewhat backward; in most countries wealth comes first *then* girls get a chance to go to school. Deuteronomy reverses this approach and makes sure that girls were educated and therefore more productive, even before they had settled in the Promised Land.

## ORPHANS AND ALIENS

The Bible regularly groups widows with orphans and aliens (or sometimes called sojourner or in modern language immigrants and/or refugees). These are three classes of people frequently on the margins and often viewed as burdens or threats. Grouping orphans with widows may seem appropriate, but grouping them with aliens may seem odd to modern thinking; modern policy debates about immigration seldom if ever include orphans and widows outside of the immigrant widows and orphans. Including native-born orphans and widows with immigrants would seem odd if not completely absurd, but throughout history these three groups have had much in common, being regularly abused and neglected by the bulk of society and frequently in official policy. To this day orphans are outcasts and considered burdens. According to the United Nations International Children's Emergency Fund (UNICEF) there are 153 million orphans in the world today,[16] however approximately 80 percent of these are classified as orphans but have a living parent, what are called single orphans while the remainder are double orphans. However, it is also largely assumed that the number of orphans is undercounted or by convention not counted. Street children are hard to estimate and those children being trafficked or serving as soldiers are very difficult to count as well. But this demonstrates the plight of orphans to this day, they are very vulnerable, subject to all sorts of abuses ranging from slave and sex trafficking to child sacrifices, which still occur in some countries:

> [I]n Uganda, where human sacrifice—especially of children—occurs despite the government's efforts to stop it . . . figures show seven child and six adult sacrifices in 2015, the most recent numbers available. In 2014, police recorded nine child and four adult sacrifices. Five years before, they counted 29 cases in total, the most in recent years.
>
> The actual number of human sacrifices likely is higher, says Kyampisi Childcare Ministries, which rehabilitates children lucky enough to escape the ritual. The organization tallied six cases this year in the capital of Kampala alone. *Thousands of children go missing in Uganda annually*, and dozens are likely victims of sacrifice, said Peter Sewakiryanga, a pastor and the aid group's director.[17] (emphasis added)

There are reports that such practices go on in many countries including Nigeria, Liberia, South Africa, Namibia, and Zimbabwe, as well as India and even in developed Western nations where some immigrants and refugees have brought pagan rituals with them.[18] In ancient Israel's time the nations regularly sacrificed children to their gods, often in the most gruesome ways imaginable.

This displays a low view of human life and an underlying attitude that a human was only as valuable as his or her direct contribution to the community's survival, which may mean sacrificing the helpless and vulnerable to benefit the wealthy and powerful. In Deuteronomy, God declares himself interested in the plight of widows, orphans, and aliens,[19] and Deuteronomy elevates them to equal social status with the priests.[20] This equality was impressive as the priests were the only elevated social class in Israel at this time, there was no royal or political institution, and while the priests had some severe limits placed on them that are discussed later, they had a high standing and respect of all the tribes. Israel was also commanded to include orphans and aliens in the celebration feasts.[21] This is significant since inclusion in the feasts was more than letting them come to the party, it implied a full citizenship status and the right to be included in all of the community's activities, they were not to be ignored or cast out or expelled and left to their own fate; Deuteronomy provided a (non-governmental) social welfare net.[22] Reinforcing this is the fact that widows, orphans, and aliens were to be given fair and equal (but not preferential) treatment before the law as well[23] and, as a sort of final statement of authority on the issue, God placed a curse on anyone who abused any of these.[24]

While orphans were and are often seen as burdens or exploitation opportunities, aliens were and are seen as threats, in several possible ways. The ongoing discussions in many countries about how to handle immigrants and refugees demonstrates that we still have not sorted out how to handle this issue. Deuteronomy does not spend much time on this issue but what it does say seems pretty clear:

"Love the sojourner, therefore, for you were sojourners in the land of Egypt."[25]

"You shall not oppress a hired servant who is poor and needy, whether he is one of your brothers or one of the sojourners who are in your land within your towns"[26]

"When you have finished paying all the tithe of your produce in the third year, which is the year of tithing, giving it to the Levite, the sojourner, the fatherless, and the widow, so that they may eat within your towns and be filled, then you shall say before the Lord your God, 'I have removed the sacred portion out of my house, and moreover, I have given it to the Levite, the sojourner, the fatherless, and the widow, according to all your commandment that you have commanded me. I have not transgressed any of your commandments, nor have I forgotten them.[27]

However, these verses just echo a running theme in the Bible about the treatment of aliens, and as Table 2.2.4 shows, there are many verses on this:

**Table 2.2.4. Verses on Aliens and Sojourners**

| *Reference* | *Verse* |
|---|---|
| Leviticus 19:34 | You shall treat the stranger who sojourns with you as the native among you, and you shall love him as yourself, for you were strangers in the land of Egypt: I am the Lord your God. |
| Exodus 23:9 | You shall not oppress a sojourner. You know the heart of a sojourner, for you were sojourners in the land of Egypt. |
| Exodus 22:1 | You shall not wrong a sojourner or oppress him, for you were sojourners in the land of Egypt. |
| Leviticus 24:22 | You shall have the same rule for the sojourner and for the native, for I am the Lord your God. |
| Psalm 146 | The Lord watches over the sojourners; he upholds the widow and the fatherless, but the way of the wicked he brings to ruin. |
| Ezekiel 47:21–23 | So you shall divide this land among you according to the tribes of Israel. You shall allot it as an inheritance for yourselves and for the sojourners who reside among you and have had children among you. They shall be to you as native-born children of Israel. With you they shall be allotted an inheritance among the tribes of Israel. In whatever tribe the sojourner resides, there you shall assign him his inheritance, declares the Lord God. |
| 1 Kings 8:41–43 | Likewise, when a foreigner, who is not of your people Israel, comes from a far country for your name's sake (for they shall hear of your great name and your mighty hand, and of your outstretched arm), when he comes and prays toward this house, hear in heaven your dwelling place and do according to all for which the foreigner calls to you, in order that all the peoples of the earth may know your name and fear you, as do your people Israel, and that they may know that this house that I have built is called by your name. |

*All verses ESV*

It should be noted that an alien could not fully participate in all aspects of Jewish society until the alien became a Jew. So, there were some restrictions, mostly in the religious aspects of community and life, but not many on the commercial side.

Aside from verses, Deuteronomy gives us an interesting and instructive example of how a non-native Israelite could integrate into Jewish society in the person of Caleb. Caleb was one of only two men from the original Egyptian Exodus (Joshua being the other) allowed to live long enough to enter the Promised Land. The original generation was cursed to die in the wilderness due to their unfaithfulness. It is common misunderstanding that the Israelites wandered for forty years, as if they did not know where they were and what they were about. They did not so much wander as take a scenic route to the Promised Land necessitated by making some key stops, the most important and famous being Mount Sinai, plus they had some diplomatic and military considerations along the way. But, for the most part, they camped, almost within sight of the Promised Land for several decades, basically waiting for people to die. Moses, for separate cause, was also not allowed to enter the Promised Land but was taken to a high point near the camp and allowed to look over into it.

Before the punishment of waiting until the older generation died off, the Israelites planned to invade and take the land. When they arrived across the Jordan River from the city of Jericho in the Promised Land they sent in twelve spies, one from each tribe, to examine the land and bring back a report. Caleb was one of the twelve spies, chosen to represent the tribe of Judah, probably the most important tribe. It was prophesied as the royal tribe in Genesis 49 as it was the tribe from which David and Solomon and Jesus came, but Caleb was not a Hebrew; he was a Kenizzite.[28] He was an alien and not just an alien but a member of a hostile nation, the Kenizzites were one of the tribes to be driven *out* of the Promised Land.[29] We are not told the full history of how Caleb came to be with the Israelites and considered part of a particular tribe, a number of possibilities exist but the fact is that aliens were not only afforded protection but could rise to prominence in Israel, even men from an enemy nation could prove themselves and be accepted in Israel.

While Deuteronomy seems to make it clear, the link between human rights and economic development seems to have been lost or ignored over the years as Western democracies sent trillions of dollars in economic development aid to tyrants and dictators who regularly oppressed their people. This approach may have begun with President Truman, who in his 1949 inaugural speech, which is commonly considered the beginning of the American aid policy and is sometimes referred to as the Four Point Speech, made an impassioned case for helping the poor people of the world develop but had a narrow focus and implied that development will lead to greater freedom:

> [w]e must embark on a bold new program for making the benefits of our scientific advances and industrial progress available for the improvement and growth of underdeveloped areas.
>
> More than half the people of the world are living in conditions approaching misery. Their food is inadequate. They are victims of disease. Their economic life is primitive and stagnant. Their poverty is a handicap and a threat both to them and to more prosperous areas.
>
> For the first time in history, humanity possesses the knowledge and skill to relieve the suffering of these people.
>
> The United States is pre-eminent among nations in the development of industrial and scientific techniques. The material resources which we can afford to use for assistance of other peoples are limited. But our imponderable resources in technical knowledge are constantly growing and are inexhaustible.
>
> I believe that we should make available to peace-loving peoples the benefits of our store of technical knowledge in order to help them realize their aspirations for a better life. And, in cooperation with other nations, we should foster capital investment in areas needing development.
>
> Our aim should be to help the free peoples of the world, through their own efforts, to produce more food, more clothing, more materials for housing, and more mechanical power to lighten their burdens.[30]

But this was a Cold War speech focused on security. President Truman made several points and sub-points about economic prosperity and does not mention the Soviet Union once, but in the end, it was clear the main goal was to defeat Communism:

> Democracy alone can supply the vitalizing force to stir the peoples of the world into triumphant action, not only against their human oppressors, but also against their ancient enemies—hunger, misery, and despair.
>
> On the basis of these four major courses of action we hope to help create the conditions that will lead eventually to personal freedom and happiness for all mankind.
>
> If we are to be successful in carrying out these policies, it is clear that we must have continued prosperity in this country and we must keep ourselves strong.
>
> Slowly but surely we are weaving a world fabric of international security and growing prosperity.
>
> We are aided by all who wish to live in freedom from fear-even by those who live today in fear under their own governments.
>
> We are aided by all who want relief from lies and propaganda-those who desire truth and sincerity.
>
> We are aided by all who desire self-government and a voice in deciding their own affairs.
>
> We are aided by all who long for economic security—for the security and abundance that men in free societies can enjoy.

> We are aided by all who desire freedom of speech, freedom of religion, and freedom to live their own lives for useful ends.
>
> Our allies are the millions who hunger and thirst after righteousness.
>
> In due time, as our stability becomes manifest, as more and more nations come to know the benefits of democracy and to participate in growing abundance, I believe that those countries which now oppose us will abandon their delusions and join with the free nations of the world in a just settlement of international differences.[31]

President Truman implies that as people get wealthier and then demand better from their government, freedom, peace and by implication human rights will spread. This is historically true, but this is the difficult path, slow and cumbersome and full of resistance. If a government wants growth, Deuteronomy makes it clear that human rights must come *first* and greater growth will follow.

The point here is not to unduly criticize President Truman, his speech, or idea, he spent much time in his speech on the value of trade, which is discussed in more detail below, and I am not doubting his desire to help the poor or the important goal of defeating Communist tyranny. But this speech set the tone for American and Western interactions with the poorer (and frequently politically unaligned) nations of the world, and it was about advancing American foreign policy interests as its first goal. That frequently meant that human rights and human dignity were secondary, or lower, considerations. Putting aside the validity of Cold War considerations, this speech and ensuing policies established a basic approach the United States and other developed nations would have toward development and poorer nations over the next seventy years; creating processes and institutions that were dependent on maintaining the government to government transfers called economic development aid even though it was well known that little of the money made it to poverty relief projects and much of it found its way to the leaders' offshore bank accounts. And, of the money that did make it to poverty relief programs, much of it failed to live up to expectations.

Deuteronomy is clear that without respect for human dignity, prosperity is impossible. President Truman said in his speech, that "Greater production is the key to prosperity and peace. And the key to greater production is a wider and more vigorous application of modern scientific and technical knowledge."[32] Deuteronomy and a significant amount of research shows that peace, true peace at the individual level, not just an absence of war, must come first and only then prosperity is possible.

This is a core idea in Deirdre McCloskey's *Bourgeois Trilogy* (2006, 2010, 2016) where she argues that a key to economic growth, the Great Enrichment as she calls the economic growth of the last few centuries, was attitudinal shifts. McCloskey argues that the extension of human dignity and respect to all members of society, not just to the landed nobility and other elites, allowed for significant economic development in pockets of Europe which became known as the Industrial Revolution, which then spread across Europe and to many of its children over the years. For McCloskey, the term *industrial revolution* is a misnomer since the first cause of the prosperous era that started in northern Europe in the seventeenth century and is still going on around the world, was not industrialization but an extension of human dignity and respect that led to accepting greater numbers of people into respectable society and, by logical extension, giving their ideas and vocations a certain respectability as well. It was this acceptance of people, ideas, and innovations that led to industrialization and eventual widespread respect for a commercial society:

> All of this [the *ancien regime*] changed on a large scale, first in Holland, in the Bourgeois Revaluation from the seventeenth through the nineteenth century. People needed to be persuaded to adopt the outcome of innovation. It was a complicated cultural task, the creation of what the great economist Joseph Schumpeter . . . called a 'business-respecting civilization'. But it did happen, and for the first time and uniquely in northwestern Europe. . . . Revaluation of the honorable transcendent, no longer confined to heroism or saintliness or courtly grace, changed society and politics. It became honorable . . . to invent a machine for making screws or to venture to in trade to Cathay. . . . That is, around 1600 on a big scale in pioneering Holland, and then around 1700 on a bigger scale, and permanently, in innovating Britain, some of the elite began to revalue the town and its vulgar and corrosive creativity.[33]

The revaluation McCloskey writes of is a rethinking of how we view man, a more Christian anthropology, something more consistent with Deuteronomy's teachings, as it was emerging in Europe. McCloskey downplays, but does not eliminate completely, the role the Reformation may have played in this revaluation but one cannot help but think of the Reformation's theological teaching of the priesthood of the believer and the underground activity (at first) of translating the Bible into the common languages, when trying to explain why "lower classes" started to be accorded respect and dignity. As Luther explained this theological principle from 1 Peter 2, it has its foundation in Exodus 19 where God calls the nation of Israel a "kingdom of Priests and a holy nation"[34] but is also reflected in the spirit of God's commands in Deuteronomy and elsewhere concerning incorporating aliens, widows, and orphans fully into society. God's political economic system does not have room for a structured class system or elitism.

William Easterly (2013, 2014), in examining modern aid-based development approaches, also argues that human rights are an essential element to economic growth and development, an idea that Easterly asserts has been largely ignored over the last fifty years. Think of the Truman speech priorities. Easterly argues that each person must be treated with dignity and respect and that much of modern political leadership in the developing world fails to do this and Western aid just reinforces this flawed approach. As he says in comments about his book *The Tyranny of Experts: Economists, Dictators, and the Forgotten Rights of the Poor*:

> The rights of the poor should be the same as the rights of the rich: the core, inalienable rights that started with the language of the Declaration of Independence, including the idea that governments exist by the consent of the governed.
>
> There is an ongoing debate around the world between the advocates of freedom for the individual and the advocates for more authoritarian, powerful states like Russia and China, and seen in battles from Ukraine to Venezuela to Ethiopia.
>
> The sad thing is that the field and practice of development have too often been on the wrong side of this debate. They've implicitly painted themselves into a corner where they're on the authoritarian side. Then they're backing the autocrats, backing the oppressors against the oppressed.
>
> I realized our attitude towards the poor is so often condescending and paternalistic. We think of them as helpless individuals. We don't respect their dignity as individuals.
>
> The next step was not to just avoid paternalism or condescension but actually to go back to first principles and think about the rights of the poor and what role those rights play in development. Economists' research actually does give the institutions associated with individual rights a lot of the credit for the development in the West and the rest of the world. This combined with my own moral awakening that these rights are a desirable good in and of themselves. Whenever we violate them, we set back development.[35]

There is a caveat that needs to be added; economic development does not require full, all-encompassing rights as we have come to know them in the modern West. This is not a more nuanced and detailed discussion of rights and what they are and how they have evolved or should evolve. The point here is that people need to be safe in their person and free to pursue their goals. It is true that even in the more advanced nations, the recognition of rights to all has come in fits and starts, there have been gender and racial issues, deep-seated classism and other issues that have hindered the full recognition of rights to all. But there is a virtuous cycle, even small steps in recognizing the rights of non-elites moves a society down the path where greater prosperity will emerge which often leads to an expansion of rights which leads to greater prosperity and then to another rights extension and so forth. We have seen this cycle in history repeat itself; as nations get wealthier, slavery is ended, minorities are treated more equally, there is equality before the law, women rise from being property to second-class citizens to full citizenship and eventually even the most marginalized are accorded full rights and respect. Deuteronomy does not discuss an evolution of expanding rights nor prescribe such an approach, it is a clean-slate approach that demands full recognition of human rights for everyone immediately because they are people who bear God's image, no other reason needed. However, this step-wise approach that many nations have followed has allowed us to see that growth and the expansion of human rights are positively correlated.

We must recognize that governments do not grant rights, they either protect them or violate them. The more universally and consistently rights are protected, the stronger the nation's economic growth tends to be. Deuteronomy may be one of the most forward-looking documents in the area of human rights and dignity. It starts with the idea that all people are created in God's image and bear his likeness. This is the basis for prohibiting murder, first established in Genesis and carried through the entire Bible. From this understanding we get a series of commands about how to treat and interact with people that reflects a high view of humans and their inherent right to respect and dignity. As the data shows, human rights and economic prosperity are strongly correlated. As the World Bank report *Human Rights and Economics: Tensions and Positive Relationships* concluded:

> Human rights add value when it comes to the quality of economic growth, and specifically the distribution of growth within a society. As such, they should not be seen as an inhibitor of economic development and growth, but rather as a framework for economic development which can inform economic policy and guide social welfare on aspects related to equity in particular.
>
> Human rights can be an effective tool for poverty reduction for three reasons: (i) Human rights contribute to empowerment and social protection of marginalized groups through social mobilization and mechanisms of strengthening accountability. (ii) Human rights reinforce the work on equity and equality by emphasizing non-discrimination. This raises a demand for disaggregate approaches and for documentation of how groups are involved and how they participate. And, (iii) human rights bring added attention to legal approaches, a feature that local actors, including state authorities themselves, are employing in social mobilization strategies.[36]

In a 2017 study called *Human Rights and Economics Growth: An Econometric Analysis of Freedom and Participation Rights*, Koob, Jorgenosn, and Sano conclude "that freedom and participation rights causes economic growth when accounting for the development of freedom and participation rights ten to fifteen years back in time, indicating that there is a long-run relationship between the two variables."[37] They further examined whether there was causality in the relationship. Contrary to President Truman's approach where prosperity created peace, Koob, et al. found that, "conclusively, the results from the Granger causality test state that the causality is strongest from freedom and participation rights to economic growth and not the other way around. . . . This gives a first indication that promoting freedom and participation rights may be the smart thing to do in terms of economic development."[38] Koob and his co-authors conclude their report by summarizing:

> . . . we find that permanent improvements in freedom and participation rights contribute positively to economic growth over the long run . . . our results provisionally indicate that economic and institutional factors may be intermediate factors of the long-run relationship. An interpretation of these results could be that strong freedom and participation rights motivate a country's population to contribute positively to the economy making them more productive as has been found and argued by Blanton and Blanton (2007a). Additionally, strong freedom and participation rights promote predictability, and economic security that encourage trade and investment that furthermore contribute to growth (Blanton and Blanton, 2007a). . . . Moreover, the results imply that there might be a cost to inaction, since a deterioration of respect for these civil and political rights seems to be harmful to economic growth.[39]

So Koob, et al. found just what Deuteronomy asserts and what McCloskey and Easterly have found; that for greatest prosperity, rights come first. While

**Table 2.2.5. Human Rights and GDP[1, 2]**

| *Country* | *Human Rights Index Score (Scale: 0-10)* | *Human Rights Abuse Risk* | *GDP per capita* | *World Rank* |
|---|---|---|---|---|
| Worst Countries | | | | |
| North Korea | .61 | Extreme | $1,700 | 215 |
| Somalia | .68 | Extreme | $400 | 230 (last) |
| Syria | .69 | Extreme | $2,900 | 194 |
| South Sudan | .82 | Extreme | $1,700 | 213 |
| Sudan | .90 | Extreme | $4,400 | 173 |
| Best Countries | | | | |
| San Marino | 8.95 | Low | $59,500 | 18 |
| Norway | 9.11 | Low | $69,200 | 13 |
| Luxembourg | 9.13 | Low | $104,000 | 4 |
| Finland | 9.26 | Low | $42,200 | 41 |
| Denmark | 9.49 | Low | $48,000 | 33 |

1. "Human Rights Risk Index 2016–Q4" (Verisk Maplecroft, December 8, 2016), https://reliefweb.int/sites/reliefweb.int/files/resources/2016_ITF_Human_Rights_Index_2016-01.pdf.
2. *The CIA World Factbook* (Washington, D.C.: United States Government, n.d.), https://www.cia.gov/library/publications/the-world-factbook/wfbExt/region_afr.html.

Table 2.2.5. is not a claim to statistical relationships or significance, it supports all that the reports referenced above have found, countries that respect people and protect human rights perform better economically than those that do not. In Table 2.2.5 are, by one measure, the five worst and five best countries on human rights and their respective per capita GDP and world rank.

Respectful treatment of women, orphans, aliens, and other marginalized people will equate in some formulaic way to economic prosperity; that is not the claim at all. But, as a consequence of treating people properly, as divine image bearers worthy of respect and dignity for that reason alone, and making that operational in full citizenship in the community allows these people, who would be marginalized outcasts, to be contributors. It gives them space to work out their creativity and ideas and contribute in whatever ways they are capable. Instead of excluding half or more of the population, grant full personhood for everyone and the growth and progress will be that much greater.

## NOTES

1. *Matthew*, n.d., 5:21–22 (ESV).
2. Cynthia Gorney, "For Widows, Life After Loss," *National Geographic*, February 2017, https://www.nationalgeographic.com/magazine/2017/02/global-images-of widows-india-bosnia-uganda-discrimination-exile/.
3. *Deuteronomy*, n.d., 10:17–18 (ESV).
4. Ibid., 26:12–16 (ESV).
5. *Malachi*, n.d., 2:16 (ESV).
6. Ibid., 2:16 (NIV).
7. Stephen P. Jenkins, "Marital Splits and Income Changes over the Longer Term" (University of Essex, U.K: Institute for Social and Economic Research, February 2008), 1, Marital splits and income changes over the longer term Stephen P. Jenkins Institute for Social and Economic Research University of Essex Colchester CO4 3 SQ p.1.
8. Ibid., 8.
9. *Deuteronomy*, 24:1 (ESV).
10. Ibid., 24:2 (ESV).
11. For a nice discussion on literacy in the ancient Near East, see *Oxford Handbook of Cuneiform Culture*, Karen Radner and Eleanor Robson (eds.). Oxford: Oxford University Press.
12. *Mark*, n.d., 10:2–9 (ESV).
13. *Mark*, n.d., 10:2–12 (ESV).
14. Shira Faigenbaum-Golovin et al., "Algorithmic Handwriting Analysis of Judah's Military Correspondence Sheds Light on Composition of Biblical Texts," *Proceedings of the National Academy of Sciences* 113, no. 17 (April 26, 2016): 4664, doi:10.1073/pnas.1522200113.

15. Kathryn Lomas et al., eds., *Literacy and the State in the Ancient Mediterranean*, Accordia Specialist Studies on the Mediterranean 7 (London: Accordia Research Institute, University of London, 2007), 37.
16. Joe Dargo, "The Hope Effect," *Are There Really 153 Million Orphans Worldwide?*, March 27, 2016, http://www.hopeeffect.com/153-million-orphans/.
17. Tony Onyulo, "In This Nation, Children's Body Parts Are Sacrificed for Witchcraft," *USA Today*, n.d.
18. Warren Manger, "Where Human Sacrifices Are Taking Place throughout the World," *The Mirror*, July 4, 2015, sec. World News.
19. *Deuteronomy*, 10:18 (ESV).
20. Ibid., 14:29; 26:12 (ESV).
21. Ibid., 16:11–14 (ESV).
22. Ibid., 24:19–21 (ESV).
23. Ibid., 24:17 (ESV).
24. Ibid., 27:19 (ESV).
25. Ibid., 10:19 (ESV).
26. Ibid., 24:14 (ESV).
27. Ibid., 26:12–13 (ESV).
28. *Joshua*, n.d., 14:6 (ESV).
29. *Genesis*, n.d., 15:18–21 (ESV).
30. "Truman's Inaugral Address" (U.S. Capitol, Washington, D.C., January 20, 1949), https://www.trumanlibrary.org/whistlestop/50yr_archive/inagural20jan1949.htm.
31. Ibid.
32. Ibid.
33. Deirdre N. McCloskey, *Bourgeois Dignity: Why Economics Can't Explain the Modern World*, Paperback ed (Chicago, Ill.: Univ. of Chicago Press, 2011), 12.
34. *Exodus*, n.d., 19:6 (ESV).
35. William Easterly, Poverty is a Moral Problem: Why Bill Gates and Rick Warren Don't Have All the Answers, April 10, 2014, https://www.redletterchristians.org/poverty-moral-problem-bill-gates-rick-warren-dont-answers/.
36. GHK Consulting Ltd., "Human Rights and Economics: Tensions and Positive Relationships" (The World Bank, 2012), 31, http://siteresources.worldbank.org/PROJECTS/Resources/40940-1331068268558/Report_Development_Fragility_Human_Rights.pdf.
37. Sigrid Alexandra Koob, Stinne Skriver Jorgenson, and Hans-Otto Sano, "Human Rights and Economic Growth: An Econometric Analysis of Freedom and Participation Rights," Matters of Concern Human Rights Research Papers (Copenhagen: The Danish Institute for Human Rights, 2017), 28, https://www.humanrights.dk/sites/humanrights.dk/files/media/dokumenter/udgivelser/research/matters_of_concern_series/final_human_rights_and_economic_growth_-_an_econometric_analysis.pdf.
38. Ibid.
39. Ibid., 38–39.

## *Chapter Three*

# Thou Shall Not Kill

## *Protection of Life against Violence*

Prohibition on murder, depending on how you count, is the seventh commandment and is possibly the most universally applied; as far as I know every society that has ever existed has had some prohibition on killing other people and punishment for violators, even if the law was selectively enforced and regularly violated in some cases. Appendix B presents a table that compares various sets of laws from the ancient Near East; the three most ancient law sets, the Laws of Ur-Nammu (2050 B.C.E.), the Code of Hammurabi (1750 B.C.E.), and the Ten Commandments (traditional dating 1440 B.C.E.), all forbid murder. But, at least for the Ten Commandments, this law is merely a brief summation of a much deeper and more complex protection of humans against all manner of violence.

Being safe in one's own person is self-evident in its economic importance. If one is under threat or at risk of violence, one does not tend to plan for the future or invest for a better tomorrow. If a person does not feel safe then all his thinking is short-term survival thinking with no development of long-term projects such as setting up a farm or business or getting an education. In extreme cases even establishing a family is not a consideration. This is obvious and well-recognized, even regimes that have questionable human rights records recognize the reality that violence is bad for a society's prospects.

While logic certainly supports the idea that violence is bad for growth and flourishing, surprisingly there are few modern cross-country studies about the effect of murder or even crime in general on economic growth. Ben Powell and his co-authors Manish and Nair offer an explanation:

> There are two general reasons why there are not more cross-country studies on how crime impacts growth. The first is that crime data are often inaccurate. The second is that what is defined as a crime in one place is not a crime in

> another, making generalizations about the effect of 'crime' on growth difficult. Even homicide, which is nearly universally illegal, is not measured consistently across countries.
>
> Cross-country data on crime are both inaccurate and inconsistent. Data gathered from official sources, i.e. from reports issued by national agencies such as the FBI, suffer from rampant underreporting. Victims often fail to report crimes to the police, especially when the offenses are minor, when certain offenses carry a social stigma as in the case of rape or domestic violence, or when victims have no faith in the authorities. Given that faith in the local authorities can vary considerably between countries and jurisdictions, variations in underreporting between countries can make meaningful cross-country comparisons difficult.
>
> The recording procedures of the various official agencies are also flawed. They may fail to include in their estimates data from all the law enforcement agencies in the country or may be selective in their recording of crimes. In El Salvador, for example, only crimes that involve an accused suspect are recorded, while the others are ignored. Japan includes a broad class of vehicular deaths in the category of homicide deaths while other countries do not. Dutch homicide rates are highly inflated when compared to those of other countries because the former include attempted homicide in their estimates. To make matters worse, the extent of these inaccuracies varies across countries. Soares (2004) finds that the extent of the reporting bias has a strong negative correlation with the level of development of a country. Thus, the extent of underreporting is found to be far larger in less developed countries where the police and judicial systems are weak. It is for these reasons that Fajnzylber et al. (2000, p. 282) state, 'one of the reasons cross-country crime studies are uncommon is that it is difficult to compare crime rates across countries.[1]

As significant as these concerns are, these limitations have not prevented some worthwhile efforts to investigate the relationship between murder and violent crime and economic growth. In September 2010 the Geneva Declaration of Armed Violence and Development released a report entitled *More Violence, Less Development*. It acknowledges the research and data collection limitations: "The collection of data on armed violence and development typically suffers from a number of selection biases. As a result, data tends to be patchy and trends are spatially and temporally uneven and possibly unrepresentative. Notwithstanding these limitations, it is possible to undertake a tentative statistical assessment of the relationships between homicidal violence and developmental progress."[2] The report provides some interesting, if not surprising findings:

- [t]he study finds that areas experiencing comparatively high rates of conflict related and homicidal violence tend to experience declining levels of progress in relation to both human development as measured by poverty, income and the achievement of specific MDG goals.

- Countries with low homicide rates make more rapid human development gains than countries with higher homicide rates. Specifically, countries featuring lower average homicide rates had a roughly 11 per cent higher chance of achieving improvement in the HDI (Human Development Index) than countries registering higher homicide rates.
- Countries reporting high levels of homicide are statistically associated with reduced progress across specific MDG Goals. Specifically, high rates of homicidal violence contributes to dramatic reductions in eradicating extreme poverty, youth unemployment and hunger (MDG 1), increased primary enrolment ratios (MDG2) and reduced infant mortality and adolescent birth rates (MDG 4 and 5);
- Meanwhile, higher levels of development tend to be associated with reduced levels of homicidal violence. Specifically, countries reporting proportionately lower levels of income inequality and unemployment feature comparatively lower levels of homicide. By way of contrast, lower levels of human development and income occurs in parallel with high and very high rates of armed violence.[3]

*Note: MDG means Millennium Development Goals, a set of eight human progress goals and measurements established by the United Nations in 2000.*

In addition to the limitations already detailed, there is the fact that these numbers can be skewed by oppressive regimes that keep murder rates low due to a large and/or secret police force but these same tactics also frequently have a significant repressive effect on economic activity. This is further complicated by how difficult it is to measure how the threat or fear of (as opposed to actual) violence may impact economic activity. Even with these measurement and research issues, it is obvious that personal violence slows economic growth. The prohibition on murder is a moral command to respect God's ultimate creation that bears His image but it is also an economic command that a people will not be prosperous if violence is allowed to go unchecked and the people are not safe to dream, invest, and build for the future.

## VIOLENCE AGAINST WOMEN

Ancient Jewish law provides a variety of protections to women and stories we have from the period tell us even more about how women were treated and the roles they had in ancient Israel, which included judge, powerful political roles, prophetess, and prominence throughout the Bible. They are both righteous and evil and it is interesting to note that several of the women given prominent roles and viewed positively were not women who many would have thought of as righteous at first glance, such as Rahab, Tamar,

Mary Magdalene, and the adulterous woman Jesus protects from stoning. The Bible, despite some modern criticisms, is very aggressive in protecting women from violence.

As basic as it may sound, the first protection of women was that they were allowed to live. To this day in many societies male babies are preferred to female ones and female babies are often killed with no moral qualms or legal penalty. As this story from 2014 about India shows:

> "As fertility declines, people choose not only the number of children they have, but also choose the sex of the child," says Poonam Muttreja, a prominent campaigner for women's rights and an adviser to the government. "And everyone wants a son."
>
> Patriarchy is so entrenched in our society. Girls are unwelcome visitor(s) in our own homes, and that's how they are treated.
>
> The skewed sex ratio is due to what Puneet Bedi, a Delhi suburb gynecologist, calls "mass murder on an unprecedented scale." Census data shows some districts in India have fewer than 800 girls born for every 1,000 boys, leaving male-heavy villages.
>
> A maverick amongst India's medical community, Bedi accuses his colleagues of helping parents use ultrasound scans to determine the sex of the baby and abort females, because of a cultural preference for sons. If this practice doesn't stop, Bedi fears the worst for the future of India.
>
> Why such a strong preference for sons exists is a matter of heated debate. Some point out that it is expensive to marry off daughters, because of the practice of dowry. Although dowry is outlawed in India, this practice persists. Others maintain that daughters only look after their in-laws, instead of their birth parents, when they grow old.
>
> Muttreja calls this pure myth. Women have been shown to be much more reliable when it comes to looking after relatives or using their earnings responsibly, she says. "While working women send money back to their families, men hold back money for liquor, cigarettes and perhaps going to sex workers, too," she says.
>
> The middle-class especially selects for sons, suggesting that economic development isn't likely to solve the problem, according to recent census data.[4]

Or this excerpt from a story about China in the same year: "A preference for boys—not least because they can earn more to support their parents—means endemic illegal sex-selective abortions and the abandonment of baby girls. The sex ratio is estimated at 120 boys for every 100 girls, far above the global average and leaving the country with 50m fewer women than men."[5] It is a tragedy to state that just surviving was a major step forward for girls and still is in many countries.

As an aside, I need to add that these policies and practices, as barbaric as they are, are in line with certain intellectuals' view that population growth is bad for economic growth and bad for the long-term, environmental sustainability of the planet. This thinking and advice, besides leading to or justifying horrendous practices primarily against girls and to some extent, disabled children, shows a complete lack of economic understanding. Killing, or preventing the thinkers and workers and creators and leaders of the next generation from being born, is one certain way to be sure we do not solve the problems we have. China is missing 50 million girls. That will change that country for the next two hundred years or more; calculating the babies they would have had and the work they would have done and ideas they would have developed just magnifies the problem. We can take that thinking and pyramid it out and realize that is a tremendous amount of talent that will never exist. And, of course, this is just part of the economic argument, the issue is so much larger and there are a significant number of so-called smart people who are complicit in this gendercide.

## RAPE

Next to actually surviving and living to adulthood, protection over one's body is the next level of human rights. Historically, sexual crime has always been a common way that men have aggressed against women. Deuteronomy deals with these issues in detail and at length. Rape was forbidden and women had legal recourse when it did happen. The first thing to recognize is that, unlike in some nations today, the woman was not to be held guilty or punished in the case of rape; "unto a (raped) maid thou shall do nothing."[6] However, circumstances and conditions required different responses. Deuteronomy 22 deals with several kinds of rape cases. Verses 23 and 24 state:

> If there is a betrothed virgin, and a man meets her in the city and lies with her, then you shall bring them both out to the gate of that city, and you shall stone them to death with stones, the young woman because she did not cry for help though she was in the city, and the man because he violated his neighbor's wife. So you shall purge the evil from your midst.[7]

Obviously, there is a spiritual element to this as the command to purge the evil is attached to these instructions but this is a tough command for moderns, that the woman, a victim of a brutal crime, would be punished with execution, seems cruel and inhumane; this is something some critics point to as proof that the Bible is not a guide for morality. Since I am claiming Deuteronomy protects women, then this instruction needs to be examined.

The first thing we must note is that the rapist is to be executed, and indeed this is the case in almost all rape punishments in Deuteronomy, the only change between the different circumstances is how the woman was to be treated. In this case there is a burden on her to seek help, to cry out, and if she does not, she is considered complicit and to be treated as a woman caught in adultery, an offense that was also punishable by execution of both parties as explained in the same chapter. While modern sensibilities may find this punishment immoral, we must look more deeply at the incentives. Adultery was a violation punishable by death, if a couple was caught the woman had every incentive to accuse the man of rape to save herself, he might even be complicit to save her since saving himself was not possible at that point, so there needed to be some evidence that there was actually a rape, and the most reliable evidence would be witnesses who could attest to the fact that she was being coerced. This ensured that true rapists were punished and that adulterous couples were not hiding behind the statute to at least save one of them from execution. For this punishment to be truly immoral and unfair, it would have to have lighter punishments for the man. While people can debate if execution is the proper punishment for this offense, the fact is that the punishment does what so many claim to want, treats men and women exactly the same.

This is not an issue just for ancients though, there is an ongoing legal debate in several countries right now about how severe the punishment should be for women who falsely accuse men of rape. England, as one example, has prosecuted over one hundred women on the charge of falsely accusing of rape in the last five years.[8] It is an issue that we have still not sorted out even thousands of years later.

In the rural areas the weight of evidence shifts, and the woman is to be believed no matter what the conditions, as is explained in verses 25 through 27 of chapter 22:

> But if in the open country a man meets a young woman who is betrothed, and the man seizes her and lies with her, then only the man who lay with her shall die. But you shall do nothing to the young woman; she has committed no offense punishable by death. For this case is like that of a man attacking and murdering his neighbor, because he met her in the open country, and though the betrothed young woman cried for help there was no one to rescue her.[9]

In this case, the woman is to be believed and the man executed. However, there is a clause we must explore, the betrothal clause. These punishments apply to a rapist of a woman who was betrothed or, as we might say, engaged to be married. If she was not betrothed, consequences were different, as verses 28 and 29 explain:

> If a man meets a virgin who is not betrothed, and seizes her and lies with her, and they are found, then the man who lay with her shall give to the father of the

> young woman fifty shekels of silver, and she shall be his wife, because he has violated her. He may not divorce her all his days.

This may be among the most controversial verses in the entire book of Deuteronomy and certainly runs against modern ideas of how rape should be handled. It sounds like a horrible punishment for the woman, to marry her rapist. But we err if we approach this with modern criminal justice and modern community relations in view.

Keeping in mind that the first goal is preventing a crime and the second is to be sure that the offender is punished and the third is that the victim is restored as best can be, this punishment is consistent. Instead of immediately dismissing this as absurd, we need to consider why this punishment is appropriate. In those days one's family was the primary way people were cared for, especially as they aged. A boy or a girl lived with their parents until they married and then would frequently live nearby or even on the same property as the husband's parents. A violated woman living in a small community as these villages were would be considered, rightly or wrongly, as un-marriageable and at risk of destitution in her dotage. She could live in her father's home until he passed and then she faced a very uncertain future. So, the penalty to marry her was a way to ensure her lifelong care, it was a lifetime penalty on the man, and in some ways more severe than the penalty for murder. In the other cases discussed above, the betrothed woman had a husband in-waiting and was only punished if she betrayed that (very serious and expensive) contract by not seeking assistance in her distress. But in this case, there is no marriage contract and she is at serious risk of destitution. The way to avoid that was to make the rapist care for her for the rest of his life. In this polygamous society, this marriage does not necessarily mean she would have to be a wife in the complete sense of the term; while that is likely it is not explicitly commanded, however, since children were also part of the social security system it is likely she would want children for many reasons, one being to care for her should the husband pass before she did. But whichever way it worked out, the man was responsible for her care until his dying day.

Data on rape is rare, a significant number of countries do not even report the statistic, which makes trying to correlate it with economic performance almost impossible. The social stigma, cultural pressure, and sheer intimidation undoubtedly suppresses and skews the numbers, significantly in some cases. In a sort of perverse backwardness some countries that actually do quite well on women's rights may look worse in the rape statistics then other nations in which women are broadly and systematically abused in all manner and forms but then the government officially lies about it in international crime and human rights reports. Victims' willingness to report rapes more frequently, knowing they stand a good chance at getting justice and less of a chance of being stigmatized leads to very skewed reporting, which is why most international lists of nations with the worst rape problems include a mix of nations all over the economic map and frequently include nations like Sri Lanka and Ethiopia as well as the United States, England, and Canada.

## SLAVES

It goes without saying that slavery is a very sensitive subject. It has divided nations and oppressed people for centuries and is largely considered one of the great human rights abuses. However, this is primarily a Western development, slavery was not widely considered wrong let alone evil and immoral until fairly recently in human history, within the past few centuries. Westerns tend to think of slavery in certain terms and certain ways that have a racial component to it, but most of the world practiced slavery that did not have a racial aspect to it at all. This is not to offer some thin justification for coercive slavery in any way, just to point out that the practice is much more broadly understood throughout history. While I do not want to minimize the form of slavery that developed in the West, as it was among the most oppressive and thankfully ended, slavery means much more and applies to many more people and for longer periods of time than what is commonly discussed in the West. This point is further illustrated by the fact that slavery is still practiced today; estimates are that as many as 30 million people are enslaved today even though it is technically illegal in every country.[10]

Slavery is also permitted in the Bible and Israel practiced it. Some point to this fact as proof the Bible is not a moral document and certainly not inspired by a loving God. Historically, others have used this as justification for their actions and beliefs in favor of slavery. Indeed, we had a strange blending of philosophies with evolution theory and biblical permissiveness giving some people personal justification for race-based slavery. These particular issues aside, the basic idea of slavery needs to be addressed if one is going to argue that the book of Deuteronomy respects human rights and elevates the human person. How can anyone make such a claim for a book that permits slavery?

*Slavery* is a loaded term. It has come to mean something in the modern world that is rightly abhorrent to civilized people, but what we know in the modern usage and recent historical sense as slavery is very different from what Deuteronomy means by slavery. The term itself comes from medieval Europe to refer to the Slavic people who were war captives of Otto the Great, the Germanic Holy Roman Emperor, and forced into servitude. But the concept has been with us for thousands of years. We must examine the biblical text free of our modern and historical baggage to truly understand what Deuteronomy means. Western slavery came to mean a mostly but not exclusively race-based practice that allowed for the holding of some people in perpetuity as property by others, including successive generations. It sometimes meant the slave was subject to punishment by the owner and open to all sorts of abuse with minimal or no penalty. That is most definitely *not* the biblical model.

First, a Hebrew slave could not be kept for more than six years without the slave's permission:

> If your brother, a Hebrew man or a Hebrew woman, is sold to you, he shall serve you six years, and in the seventh year you shall let him go free from you. And when you let him go free from you, you shall not let him go empty-handed. You shall furnish him liberally out of your flock, out of your threshing floor, and out of your winepress. As the LORD your God has blessed you, you shall give to him.[11]

While the way in which a Hebrew might become a slave is not discussed in this passage, the original language allows for the possibility that a person might sell himself into slavery. The length of time of service is set and the service terminates with the slave leaving with significant assets. This was less like slavery and more like a contract of indentured servitude, something common into the relatively modern era. Deuteronomy does not leave the issue there however:

> You shall remember that you were a slave in the land of Egypt, and the LORD your God redeemed you; therefore I command you this today. But if he [slave] says to you, 'I will not go out from you,' because he loves you and your household, since he is well-off with you, then you shall take an awl, and put it through his ear into the door, and he shall be your slave forever. And to your female slave you shall do the same. It shall not seem hard to you when you let him go free from you, for at half the cost of a hired worker he has served you six years. So the LORD your God will bless you in all that you do.[12]

The term of service could continue and even become permanent but only if the slave agreed and, as we learn in Exodus 21, the agreement had to be witnessed by officials. But the fact that this was a possibility indicates that the expectation was that conditions and the services were not harsh and unjust, that these slaves were to be treated like humans and not beasts of burden, and that the terms and conditions could be agreeable enough that the servant would desire to stay.

Exodus 21 gives us some other insights on slavery in ancient Israel. Exodus 21:16 states, "Whoever steals a man and sells him, and anyone found in possession of him, shall be put to death."[13] This is another significant distinction between modern and recent slavery practices and how it was practiced in ancient Israel, there was to be no capturing of people for the sole purpose of selling them into slavery. This was a capital crime. The slave trade as it developed in Europe and the Americas and as it is practiced in some places today was completely wrong based on biblical standards and the traders would have been executed in ancient Israel. Exodus 21 goes on to provide slaves protection against abuse:

> When a man strikes his slave, male or female, with a rod and the slave dies under his hand, he shall be avenged . . . When a man strikes the eye of his slave, male or female, and destroys it, he shall let the slave go free because of his eye. If he knocks out the tooth of his slave, male or female, he shall let the slave go free because of his tooth.[14]

Furthermore, Deuteronomy grants slaves access to the justice system and they were to be treated as any free person in the courts. This law is commonly thought to refer to foreign-born slaves since Jewish slaves were already explicitly granted these protections and access to the courts. Some scholars think that this treatment of slaves, combined with the fact that escaped slaves were not automatically returned to their masters and were granted freedom to live and to be left alone,[15] established Israel as a safe haven where the least of society and surrounding societies would be granted asylum and given justice in their cause.[16]

## SOME TROUBLING VERSES ON SLAVERY

While all that I have written above is true, and there were rules and regulations about the treatment of slaves and servants, especially Hebrew slaves who most likely sold themselves into that condition probably due to desperation and hard financial distress, there are some difficult verses as well. I would be remiss and dishonest not to deal with some of the other verses on slavery that trouble people. If I am going to claim that Deuteronomy elevates the human person, we have to deal with all of it and not cherry-pick the favorable verses.

Before I examine these verses, I need to remind the reader of something I wrote earlier, that there is a spiritual purpose to Deuteronomy and aspects of this book that do not apply to modern secular nations but did apply to Israel whose operating assumption was that it was a special people chosen by God for a special purpose. I am not hiding behind this caveat to avoid hard verses, but we need to examine the book honestly with its original purposes in mind. It is a book to help develop a people into a prosperous nation, but it is also a book to develop a people into a pure and holy nation set aside for the purpose of being God's example on earth, which meant it was to be different from any other nation past, present, or future, as Deuteronomy clearly states: "For you are a people holy to the LORD your God. The LORD your God has chosen you to be a people for his treasured possession, out of all the peoples who are on the face of the earth."[17]

That said, I quoted a verse above from Exodus 21 about how if a master kills a slave then the master would face justice, however there is more to the verse. Some may point out that in verse 21 of Exodus 21, a master is not to face any punishment if he beats his slave and the slave lives, even if the slave is injured: "But if the slave survives a day or two, he is not to be avenged, for the slave is his money [property]."[18] There are two ways to evaluate this verse. One way is against a modern standard of justice. That leads to a valuable and involved discussion about where we get such standards of justice and how we reach agreement to those standards and so forth. This is an extremely important discussion and many volumes have been filled on it; reviewing all the arguments and points is beyond my scope and purpose. However, some theologians make a spiritual and civil distinction on this verse, that the master is not to be criminally or civilly punished but he has committed a crime before God and justice will be done. As the Protestant Reformer John Calvin wrote in commenting on this verse:

> And if a man smite his servant. Although in civil matters there was a wide distinction between slaves and free-men, still, that God may show how dear and precious men's lives are to Him, He has no respect to persons with regard to murder; but avenges the death of a slave and a free-man in the same way, if he should die immediately of his wound. Indeed, it was a proof of gross barbarism amongst the Romans and other nations, to give to masters the power of life and death; for men are bound together by a more sacred tie, than that it should be permitted to a master to kill with impunity his wretched slave; nor are some men so set over others, as that they should exercise tyranny, or robbery, neither does reason permit that any private individual should usurp to himself the power of the sword. But, although unjust cruelty was not prohibited, as it should have been, by the laws of Rome, yet they confessed that slaves should be used like hired servants. The exception, which immediately follows, does not seem very consistent, for, if the slave should die after some time, the penalty of murder is remitted; whereas it would often be preferable to die at once of a single wound, than to perish by a lingering illness; and it might happen that the slave should be so bruised and maimed by blows, as to die some time afterwards. In this ease, the cruelty of the master would be surely greater than if he had committed the murder under the impulse of burning anger: wherefore the enactment appears to be a very unjust one. But it must be remarked, that the murder of those slaves, who had been obliged to take to their bed from their wounds, was not

> unpunished. Whence we gather, that it was not allowable for cruel and truculent masters to wound their slaves severely; and this is what the words expressly imply, for the smiter is only exempted from punishment when he shall have so restrained himself as that the marks of his cruelty should not appear. For that the slaves should "stand for one or two days," is equivalent to saying, that they were perfect and sound in all their members; but if a wound had been inflicted, or there was any mutilation, the smiter was guilty of murder. None, therefore, is absolved but he who only meant to chastise his slave; and where no injury appears, it is probable that there was no intention to kill him. Whilst, then, this law prohibits bloodthirsty assaults, it by no means gives greater license to murder. The reason, which is added, must be restricted to the private loss; because a murderer would never be absolved on the pretext that he had purchased his slave with money, since the life of a man cannot be so estimated.[19]

In other words, for criminal and civil purposes the verse makes a distinction between kinds of murder. Willful and deliberate murder, of anyone, even a slave, was punishable as a capital offense. This is what some countries may call a first-degree murder. However, a victim who takes several days to die was most likely not deliberately murdered. The death was an accident and not intended. Modern criminal justice makes such distinctions, referring to this a second-degree murder or manslaughter and the penalty is less than for first-degree murder. And that was the case here. One can debate if the penalty, the loss of the value of slave, seems appropriate, but that is a different discussion.

The other way to evaluate this penalty is by the standards of the law of the time. Does the law treat the accidental death of a slave differently than the accidental death or beating of a free person? Exodus 21 deals with these issues as well. In verses 18–19 the penalty for beating a free man who did not die was to pay for his medical care. Presumably, the owner of a beaten slave would pay for his medical care or at least have been without his services during a healing period, so there seems to be some equity in this penalty. In verses 28–30 we see that if an ox escaped and killed a man, the penalty was a fine and the ox was to be killed, unless the ox was known to be dangerous then the owner was to be executed as well. So, in two cases we see that accidental death was not punishable by more than a monetary penalty even between free people. In this sense the slave was being given equivalent justice, and his dignity and human rights were as respected as everyone else's.

## WAR

Another very complex area is war. Christian thinkers of all sorts have wrestled with Just War theories and acceptable conduct in war at both the policy level and the individual combatant level. Given human proclivities to engage in this activity, it is a vital topic. Deuteronomy 20:10–15 deals with how to handle war, and specifically captured prisoners.

> When you draw near to a city to fight against it, offer terms of peace to it. And if it responds to you peaceably and it opens to you, then all the people who are found in it shall do forced labor for you and shall serve you. But if it makes no peace with you, but makes war against you, then you shall besiege it. And when the Lord your God gives it into your hand, you shall put all its males to the sword, but the women and the little ones, the livestock, and everything else in the city, all its spoil, you shall take as plunder for yourselves. And you shall enjoy the spoil of your enemies, which the Lord your God has given you. Thus you shall do to all the cities that are very far from you, which are not cities of the nations here.[20]

The Israelites were commanded to offer terms to any city they came up against and if the city agreed then the people of that city would be captives and serve as forced labor, but if the city refused terms, then the city was to be destroyed and all males killed but the women, children, and assets could be preserved as war spoils. This sounds vicious and at odds with a number of commands found elsewhere in the Bible about loving thy neighbor and enemy. War is not pretty but is sometimes necessary. However, war was not the way the Israelites were supposed to live, unlike several neighboring empires for whom war was a primary activity. There was to be a period of conquest and settlement and then largely peace and trade, more on this later. Israel was not supposed to be an aggressor nation; indeed Deuteronomy 17 makes specific provisions against Israel having a large standing army, it was only to raise an army as needed. So, while not explicitly stated in these verses, the context points to the operating assumption that these verses, at least after the conquest, refer to acts of defense or responses to a previous aggression by the city in question.

There is a significant clause in this passage that many modern critics and scholars might dismiss or overlook, but should not. When Israel went to war it was only at the clear direction of God. If this was an unjust war, then Israel was destined to lose; even if the war was just but done in a way out of God's purview, Israel would lose. The modern enlightened mind dismisses this clause; after all, every advancing army claims some god is on its side, but to a faithful, God-fearing people this was a significant consideration in making a war decision. Israel had lost an unjust battle before, as told in Numbers 14 and retold in Deuteronomy 1, and it would happen again in Joshua and quite a bit during the monarchy years. These were not after-the-fact conclusions of 'we lost, so God must not have been with us' but frequently forewarned in more of prophecy of 'God is not with you, you will lose.' Israel's political and military leaders had a very real constraint on how and when they conducted war which is why even in its apex of power and wealth, the nation never sought to expand territory by conquest.

In conjunction with not being a warlike nation, by the standards of the day, these terms in Deuteronomy 20 were generous. The Assyrians particularly but also others were much more vicious, cruel, and aggressive, engaging in all sorts of inhumane tortures, destruction, and brutality. Contrary to the way the surrounding nations conducted war, Deuteronomy tied victory in war to obedience to God which means that the way Israel was treating its people, including the poor and slaves, impacted battle outcomes. "Sin in the camp" was a reason for loss in battle. That is not to say that these rules were absolutely followed, but the battle loss of Israel at Ai as told in Joshua 7 due to what some may consider small levels of disobedience is telling as to how serious "sin in the camp" was considered.

There is the rest of Deuteronomy 20 to consider. In verses 16 through 18 we read:

> But in the cities of these peoples that the Lord your God is giving you for an inheritance, you shall save alive nothing that breathes, but you shall devote them to complete destruction, the Hittites and the Amorites, the Canaanites and the Perizzites, the Hivites and the Jebusites, as the Lord your God has commanded, that they may not teach you to do according to all their abominable practices that they have done for their gods, and so you sin against the Lord your God.[21]

The verses above are actually a bit of a summary of a previous passage:

> When the Lord your God brings you into the land that you are entering to take possession of it, and clears away many nations before you, the Hittites, the Girgashites, the Amorites, the Canaanites, the Perizzites, the Hivites, and the Jebusites, seven nations more numerous and mightier than you, and when the Lord your God gives them over to you, and you defeat them, then you must devote them to complete destruction. You shall make no covenant with them and show no mercy to them. You shall not intermarry with them, giving your daughters to their sons or taking their daughters for your sons, for they would turn away your sons from following me, to serve other gods. Then the anger of the Lord would be kindled against you, and he would destroy you quickly. But thus shall you deal with them: you shall break down their altars and dash in pieces their pillars and chop down their Asherim and burn their carved images with fire.[22]

While the command "no quarter" has been given in war throughout history, these instructions seem harsh to the modern ear and they are. This is also one of those commands that has more specific spiritual weight and is not broadly applicable to any other nation or situation, not then or now or any time in between. Now, you may be saying that is convenient, take a hard verse that runs at odds with your theses and just throw it out as not applying. I agree but allow me my apologia on this if you will.

Deuteronomy 7 clearly puts this command in the spiritual realm. This was an act of spiritual purity Israel was to follow in order to be what God wanted them to be, an instrument of His judgment on the people living in Canaan. We get a first glimpse of this in Genesis 15 when God tells Abraham the inhabitants of the land of Canaan had not yet completed their evil, that is, God was going to give them more time, but they were not going to repent and they would be punished and that God would use Abraham's descendants (Israel) to punish them. Deuteronomy 18 reiterates the spiritual danger these nations posed to Israel when in verse 9 Moses commands Israel not to go after the "abominations of those nations" and then goes on to list what these abominations were.

Maybe the most definitive statements on the purpose and nature of the command to utterly destroy and kill all is a two-part statement. In Deuteronomy 9, Moses reminds the nation of who they are and what they are:

> Do not say in your heart, after the Lord your God has thrust them out before you, 'It is because of my righteousness that the Lord has brought me in to possess this land,' whereas it is because of the wickedness of these nations that the Lord is driving them out before you. Not because of your righteousness or the uprightness of your heart are you going in to possess their land, but because of the wickedness of these nations the Lord your God is driving them out from before you, and that he may confirm the word that the Lord swore to your fathers, to Abraham, to Isaac, and to Jacob.
>
> Know, therefore, that the Lord your God is not giving you this good land to possess because of your righteousness, for you are a stubborn people. Remember and do not forget how you provoked the Lord your God to wrath in the wilderness. From the day you came out of the land of Egypt until you came to this place, you have been rebellious against the Lord.[23]

They were getting the land, not because they deserved it, but because the evil of the inhabitants was full, as mentioned in Genesis 15, and it was time for judgment. Israel was not a particularly deserving group. But God is just and fair and *before* He told the Israelites to destroy the people, He warned them they were next. In Numbers 33 we read:

> And the Lord spoke to Moses in the plains of Moab by the Jordan at Jericho, saying, "Speak to the people of Israel and say to them, When you pass over the

> Jordan into the land of Canaan, then you shall drive out all the inhabitants of the land from before you and destroy all their figured stones and destroy all their metal images and demolish all their high places. And you shall take possession of the land and settle in it, for I have given the land to you to possess it. You shall inherit the land by lot according to your clans. To a large tribe you shall give a large inheritance, and to a small tribe you shall give a small inheritance. Wherever the lot falls for anyone, that shall be his. According to the tribes of your fathers you shall inherit. But if you do not drive out the inhabitants of the land from before you, then those of them whom you let remain shall be as barbs in your eyes and thorns in your sides, and they shall trouble you in the land where you dwell. *And I will do to you as I thought to do to them.*"[24] (emphasis added)

God punishes evil, no matter who does it, and as we see later, as God sends repeated warnings to Israel and after the split kingdom to Judah as well of coming judgment in the form of foreign invaders which happens on several occasions with the Assyrians and Babylonians figuring prominently.

I have spent quite a bit of time discussing war and its after-affects, but one thing that needs to be pointed out is that in the overall balance, not much of the Old Testament is spent on war and conquest stories. When one tours the British Museum or other displays, the walls are lined with stone reliefs telling the tales of conquest and victory of ancient civilizations. War is the dominant theme in many of these pictorial histories; even in more recent times, tales such as the Bayeux Tapestry stories are all about war victories, indeed there are some leaders and civilizations that the bulk of what we know about them come from pictorial war histories. For instance we are still uncertain how Alexander the Great died. The Old Testament is much different, a relatively small part are war stories and of the ones that are told, a significant portion are losses. There are approximately ninety battle stories in the Old Testament, several are of civil wars and only forty-six are of victories. Israel did not have a vaunted and feared military tradition, it was not who they were or who they were supposed to be and when they tried outside of God's direction they lost, regularly. As one scholar puts it, "We need to see [that], *the aftermath of Joshua's victories are featherweight descriptions in comparison to those found in the annals of the ancient Near East's major empires*—whether Hittite and Egyptian (second millennium), Aramaean, Assyrian, Babylonian, Persian, or Greek (first millennium). Unlike Joshua's brief, four-verse description of the treatment of the five kings (10:24–27), Assyrians were experts at rape and pillage."[25]

The temptation is to close this section with a discussion of biblical justifications for war and rules of war conduct applied to the modern age. That is not the purpose of this book, and it is a topic I cannot do justice to at the tail end of a single chapter. There are some very good works on this starting with Augustine for the interested student.

## SUMMARY

Deuteronomy and the supporting writings elevate the human person to a degree that no other society did then and many still do not today. Women, orphans, aliens, slaves, and prisoners were accorded respect and dignity based solely on being a person, regardless of status or wealth. A person's place in life did not dictate if he or she had any rights.

The modern world is still dealing with these issues. As of this writing there is a significant global refugee issue, which ebbs and flows but never really goes away. It is a hotly debated political topic in the United States and elsewhere. There is an orphan issue, which includes international adoption efforts but also, at its darkest, is also a child prostitution and human trafficking issue. Studies suggest that there are 68.5 million people who are forcibly displaced and of those 25 million are full-fledged refugees at one time[26] and 600,000–800,000 children (and young women) are human trafficking victims, with about 80 percent being trafficked for sexual exploitation purposes.[27] Women's rights are not respected, they are facing genital mutilation, severe ostracism, honor killings by family members, trafficking, and less threatening but equally oppressive prohibitions on attending school and being treated like property. All of this is counter to Deuteronomy and highly depressive on growth outcomes. When people, created in the image of God with creative capacity to solve problems and serve others, are prevented from doing so, there is no benefit to anyone and flourishing will be hindered.

No nation lives up to the standard of full equality before the law for all. Even the terms get distorted and abused and misused for political purposes. There are improvements possible everywhere but better human rights and the effort to treat everyone equally coincides with wealth and prosperity. Deuteronomy establishes an equality of all people before God and the Law in the land of Israel. It does not assume equal ability nor state that equality of outcomes is expected, there were wealthy and poor, but from the king and the high priest to the foreign-born slave, all were to be accorded the same respect as a person created in God's image and as an equal before the law. People are not burdens, but the creative engines that improve life and create flourishing. Deuteronomy is the first political document to realize this truth fully and put it into action.

## NOTES

1. Bruce L Benson and Paul R Zimmerman, *Handbook on the Economics of Crime* (Cheltenham, UK; Northampton, MA: Edward Elgar, 2010), 336, http://public.eblib.com/choice/publicfullrecord.aspx?p=599662.

2. Julie Abbass et al., "More Violence, Less Development," Declaration (Geneva, September 2010), 10, http://www.genevadeclaration.org/fileadmin/docs/MDG_Process/MoreViolenceLessDevelopment.pdf.

3. Ibid., 9–10.

4. Carl Gierstorfer, "While India's Girls Are Aborted, Brides Are Wanted," *CNN Freedom Project*, September 3, 2014, http://www.cnn.com/2014/09/03/world/asia/india-freedom-project/index.html.

5. "Why China's Boom May Be Coming to an End—and the 50 Million Women Shortage Is to Blame," December 2, 2013, https://www.telegraph.co.uk/news/worldnews/asia/china/10484993/Why-Chinas-boom-may-be-coming-to-an-end-and-the-50-million-women-shortage-is-to-blame.html.

6. *Deuteronomy*, n.d., 22:26 (ESV).

7. Ibid., 22:23–24 (ESV).

8. Sandra Laville, "109 Women Proesecuted for False Rape Claims in Five Years, Say Campaigners," *The Guardian*, December 1, 2014, sec. UK Politics, https://www.theguardian.com/law/2014/dec/01/109-women-prosecuted-false-rape-allegations.

9. *Deuteronomy*, 22:25–27 (ESV).

10. Max Fisher, "This Map Shows Where the World's 30 Million Slaves Live. There Are 60,000 in the U.S.," *Washington Post*, October 17, 2013, https://www.washingtonpost.com/news/worldviews/wp/2013/10/17/this-map-shows-where-the-worlds-30-million-slaves-live-there-are-60000-in-the-u-s/?noredirect=on&utm_term=.cd51f2e602e7.

11. *Deuteronomy*, 15:12–15 (ESV).

12. Ibid., 15:16–18 (ESV).

13. *Exodus*, n.d., 21:16 (ESV).

14. Ibid., 21:16–20 (ESV).

15. *Deuteronomy*, 23:15–16 (ESV).

16. Henry, Matthew. *The Exposition of the Old and New Testaments.* Volume I. 1706. In his commentary Henry expands on the point: "We cannot suppose that they were hereby obliged to give entertainment to all the unprincipled men that ran from service; Israel needed not (as Rome at first did) to be thus peopled. But, 1. They must not deliver up the trembling servant to his enraged master, till upon trial it appeared that the servant has wronged his master and was justly liable to punishment. Note, It is an honourable thing to shelter and protect the weak, provided they be not wicked."

17. *Deuteronomy*, 7:6 (ESV).

18. *Exodus*, 21:21 (ESV).

19. Jean Calvin et al., *Calvin's Commentaries.* (Grand Rapids, Mich.: Baker Books, 2009), Vol. 2.

20. *Deuteronomy*, 20:10–15 (ESV).

21. Deuteronomy 20:16–18 (ESV).

22. *Deuteronomy*, 7:1–6 (ESV).
23. Ibid., 9:4–7 (ESV).
24. *Numbers*, n.d., 33:50–56 (ESV).
25. Paul Copan, “How Could God Command Killing the Canaanites?” *Enrichment Journal*, Fall 2010.
26. “Figures at a Glance” (United Nations High Commissioner for Refugees, 2017), https://www.unhcr.org/figures-at-a-glance.html.
27. United States State Department, “Trafficking in Person Report” (Washington, D.C., June 2004), 7, http://www.state.gov/documents/organization/34158.pdf.

## *Chapter Four*

# Thou Shall Not Steal

## *Property Rights*

Perhaps no issue has caused more controversy in the social sciences and the moral sciences than that of property. Marxists and fellow travelers argue that private property has been the tool or enabling mechanism for the rise of classes and the oppression of the poor and that humans will never be free until the notion of private property rights is abolished. Others have not gone quite this far but certainly believe that restrictions, regulations, and controls on private property are essential for a fair and just society. Ideas emanating from the social democracy school of thought argue that private property is acceptable to an extent but that society should be able to influence or even control its use, presumably through voting.

Of course, this investigation is about the biblical model, not others' unfortunate and misguided response to it. Frequently we think of Exodus as the first place where property is discussed in the prohibition on theft, but that is not the case. Exodus begins the process of embedding private property into the moral order and codifying it in civil law but the concept predates the Ten Commandments by centuries. While many aspects of the original arrangement in the Garden of Eden are opaque to us, by chapter 4 of Genesis we learn that the institution of private property had emerged. Cain and Abel brought offerings to the Lord out of their harvest, the fruits of their efforts from raising crops (Cain) and sheep (Abel). I return to the other economic implications of the sacrifice system in a later chapter, but an offering or sacrifice makes no sense outside of the institution of private property. It is no sacrifice or act of faith to forgo the use of a communal sheep or harvest.

We see incidents of private property throughout the Pentateuch with the patriarchs; Abraham buys a burial tomb for his wife Sarah in Genesis 23, Jacob sells his labor and services to Laban in Genesis 29, and in Genesis 30

Jacob and Laban divide ownership of a large flock and Jacob buys some land in Genesis 33. These are but some of numerous examples of private property and exchange. In these examples, one party of each of these transactions was not part of Abraham's family, not subject to the commands and traditions that would later become part of Israel's identity, demonstrating that private property ownership and exchange is not the domain of a few cultural or religious traditions. Ownership of property is natural and was widely practiced from the beginning. But understanding that what may seem natural and even practiced by God's chosen may not actually be God's way (see Solomon's many wives, David's personal issues), we look for verification that private property is truly part of the moral order. God establishes His views on property ownership early on in Genesis 15, when He uses private property language:

> After these things the word of the Lord came to Abram in a vision: "Fear not, Abram, I am your shield; your reward shall be very great." . . . And he said to him, "I am the Lord who brought you out from Ur of the Chaldeans to *give you this land to possess*." But he said, "O Lord God, how am I to know that *I shall possess it*?" . . . the Lord said to Abram, "Know for certain that your offspring will be sojourners in a land that is not theirs and will be servants there, and they will be afflicted for four hundred years. But I will bring judgment on the nation that they serve, and afterward *they shall come out with great possessions*. As for you, you shall go to your fathers in peace; you shall be buried in a good old age. And they shall come back here in the fourth generation, for the iniquity of the Amorites is not yet complete." On that day the Lord made a covenant with Abram, saying, "*To your offspring I give this land, from the river of Egypt to the great river, the river Euphrates*, the land of the Kenites, the Kenizzites, the Kadmonites, the Hittites, the Perizzites, the Rephaim, the Amorites, the Canaanites, the Girgashites and the Jebusites."[1] (emphasis added)

God is quite comfortable with private property and possession, both in terms of owning land and other material possessions. As the passage above implies, the entire Jewish economy is based on private property ownership, which is a main reason the land would flow with milk and honey.

Deuteronomy uses very strong language and examples to expand and extend our understanding of private property. We see the concept reinforced throughout the Bible, verifying that God supports and protects private property ownership and that it was not just a temporary institution for a specific period of time. Deuteronomy stands diametrically opposed to any notion that communal property is in any way compatible with flourishing and prosperity, and even scholars who are skeptical that the Bible supports a free market system acknowledge that the Bible supports private property: "private property is enshrined as a fundamental good and a right for the children of Israel."[2]

It can and has been argued that property ownership is natural. Without delving too deeply into Natural Law Theory we do see the idea of property ownership discussed favorably by both Locke and Rousseau, even though they disagreed on some particulars and they both extended the concept well beyond land. But even extending beyond the Natural Law theorists and looking at nature itself we see the idea of property. Animals of all sorts from high mammals to low invertebrates defend their territory. In many cases trespassing animals know that they are violating another's territory. The notion of mine and thine does not have to be taught or explained, the Bible assumes it as well, there is never a passage that explains the basis or private property, just verses defending it.

## OWNING LAND

The first thing many people think of in a property rights discussion is land, and that makes sense, since we all live on a patch of land and we understand the concept intuitively. Israel was an agrarian-based economy, as are most developing nations and as was every society until relatively recently. As little as a hundred years ago a third of Americans lived and worked on a farm. So, it is from the idea of land and its use from which we develop property protection. Land property was of the utmost importance and Deuteronomy spends quite a bit of time on the topic which sets the tone and provides the guidelines for how other sorts of property should be treated.

The importance of land is made clear in Deuteronomy 19, a chapter dealing with legal issues like cities of refuge and witnesses for a trial. There is this one verse, verse 14: "You shall not move your neighbor's landmark, which the men of old have set, in the inheritance that you will hold in the land that the Lord your God is giving you to possess."[3] The placement of the verse seems odd and it stands alone with no other context or discussion of property, but it is placed in a chapter (note: the chapter and verse designations were established much later) dealing with some very important legal issues which implies that moving property markers was a serious offense and has both spiritual and temporal implications. Leaving the spiritual implications for others, the temporal issue is that this is a criminal offense which is a form of stealing. Deuteronomy, by its placement in this section, makes a violation of land property rights equivalent to the offense of being a false witness, discussed in verses immediately following this one, and murder, discussed in the verses immediately preceding this one. There is no criminal penalty listed for moving a property marker, but the penalty for murder was death and the penalty for being a false witness was whatever the penalty would have been to the one falsely accused if the charges had been true. The context makes it clear that all of these are crimes of deception. The specific kind of murder dealt with here was an ambush attack which is called an evil that needed to be eradicated from the nation.

## OTHER PROPERTY

But the Scriptures do not leave it at land property boundaries. There is a much more detailed discussion about property protections in the book of Exodus:

> If a man steals an ox or a sheep, and kills it or sells it, he shall repay five oxen for an ox, and four sheep for a sheep. If a thief is found breaking in and is struck so that he dies, there shall be no bloodguilt for him, but if the sun has risen on him, there shall be bloodguilt for him. He shall surely pay. If he has nothing, then he shall be sold for his theft. If the stolen beast is found alive in his possession, whether it is an ox or a donkey or a sheep, he shall pay double. If a man causes a field or vineyard to be grazed over, or lets his beast loose and it feeds in another man's field, he shall make restitution from the best in his own field and in his own vineyard. If fire breaks out and catches in thorns so that the stacked grain or the standing grain or the field is consumed, he who started the fire shall make full restitution. If a man gives to his neighbor money or goods to keep safe, and it is stolen from the man's house, then, if the thief is found, he shall pay double. If the thief is not found, the owner of the house shall come near to God to show whether or not he has put his hand to his neighbor's property. For every breach of trust, whether it is for an ox, for a donkey, for a sheep, for a cloak, or for any kind of lost thing, of which one says, 'This is it,' the case of both parties shall come before God. The one whom God condemns shall pay double to his neighbor. If a man gives to his neighbor a donkey or an ox or a sheep or any beast to keep safe, and it dies or is injured or is driven away, without anyone seeing it, an oath by the Lord shall be between them both to see whether or not he has put his hand to his neighbor's property. The owner shall accept the oath, and he shall not make restitution. But if it is stolen from him, he shall make restitution to its owner. If it is torn by beasts, let him bring it as evidence. He shall not make restitution for what has been torn. If a man borrows anything of his neighbor, and it is injured or dies, the owner not being with it, he shall make full restitution. If the owner was with it, he shall not make restitution; if it was hired, it came for its hiring fee.[4]

There is much in this passage, but there is one overarching point; private property is important. It is so well and heavily protected that one can conclude it is a necessary condition for prosperity and flourishing. Violating private property rights came with severe punishments although they differ depending on the violation, and there are several principles worth exploring in this passage.

The first principle is that the punishments are significant but varied. They range from the thief making full restitution to being sold into slavery. The justice system is discussed in a later chapter, but the goal of making restitution to the victim is the anchor of the entire array of punishments for property crime and negligence. The willful destruction or disposal of stolen property carried the harshest punishment, requiring a fivefold or fourfold restitution. This may seem excessive, but keep in mind the goal was to discourage theft, not make it more palatable should one get caught. However, what we see in this punishment is also the recognition of what economists call opportunity cost. If one has his ox stolen, that was a significant loss that placed a huge burden on the farmer and the other beasts, as that ox's work as a beast of burden was lost and had to be performed in some other way. The point is it was not just a lost animal, it was lost production, the farmer had lost a key factor of production by which he fed his family, and the punishment builds that concept into it.

Smaller animals like sheep had a different role. They were far less likely to be beasts of burden and were productive in a different way. Still very important, a four-to-one ratio is no small thing, but these sorts of animals did little work and were unlikely to put the farmer in immediate hardship, although years later when the prophet Nathan uses the parable of a stolen sheep to show King David his sin with Bathsheba, David was prepared to punish the thief severely and the fourfold restitution was part of it (2 Samuel 12). But the sheep produces milk and wool for consumption for the market and while it does impose a burden on the family having to go without, it is a smaller animal and the farmer was likely to have more than one. In both cases, though, the recognition of lost use, inconvenience, and the creation of a burden on the family are embedded in the punishment.

The second principle is that property owners have full authority to protect their property. A thief takes on the full responsibility of his actions and the owner is within his rights to kill the thief, however there is an interesting clause. If the thief is killed then the burden of restitution does not fall on anyone else, the owner does not get to kill the thief and collect damages from his family. Presumably a thief killed in the act would not have successfully stolen anything, but it is possible to have destroyed some property. However, if the thief did get away with the crime and is caught later he must make double restitution if he still has the stolen property and be sold into slavery if he cannot pay the bill. Restitution is still the main punishment for the crime, being sold into slavery is not a punishment for stealing but a final recourse to satisfy the restitution requirement.

A third principle is that negligence requires restitution. It is not the same as theft but still carries a responsibility. The examples of an out-of-control fire or a loose animal are certainly not exhaustive, but any property destroyed as a result of negligence must be restored fully although there is no additional restitution required. While the opportunity costs in this case can be just as high as in the stolen and destroyed/sold ox situation, a negligence issue should be easier and more quickly resolved, as the parties are not trying to avoid being caught and the event is more openly known. Plus, there is no disincentive necessary to build into this situation, full restitution is enough.

A fourth principle is that there are acts that cannot be avoided, what we might ironically refer to as Acts of God, and these should be treated differently. If a person borrows some property or rents some property, he is responsible for it unless it was a situation that even proper diligence and care could not prevent.

Another principle contained in this passage is that property is broadly defined. This passage lists several kinds of property that can be lost or stolen: ox, donkey, sheep, cloak, or "any kind of lost thing." Obviously this is open-ended and can refer to any tangible item that can be physically lost or stolen. In this context land is excluded since it is very difficult to lose or steal land except by false boundary markers. Other verses extend the property concept to labor and wages: "You shall not oppress a hired servant who is poor and needy, whether he is one of your brothers or one of the sojourners who are in your land within your towns. You shall give him his wages on the same day, before the sun sets. . . ."[5] The worker has sold his labor to an employer and like any other transfer of value, he is entitled to full payment when the transaction is completed. This verse has numerous applications for employers and workers but the clear indication is that the labor and time belong to the worker and he sold it to the employer and is entitled to his payment.

A passage from Exodus reinforces this idea as well and even touches on the idea of intellectual property:

> The LORD said to Moses, "See, I have called by name Bezalel the son of Uri, son of Hur, of the tribe of Judah, *and I have filled him with the Spirit of God, with ability and intelligence, with knowledge and all craftsmanship, to devise artistic designs, to work in gold, silver, and bronze, in cutting stones for setting, and in carving wood, to work in every craft.* And behold, I have appointed with him Oholiab, the son of Ahisamach, of the tribe of Dan. And I have given to all able men ability, that they may make all that I have commanded you: the tent of meeting, and the ark of the testimony, and the mercy seat that is on it, and all the furnishings of the tent, the table and its utensils, and the pure lampstand with all its utensils, and the altar of incense, and the altar of burnt offering with all its utensils, and the basin and its stand, and the finely worked garments, the

> holy garments for Aaron the priest and the garments of his sons, for their service as priests, and the anointing oil and the fragrant incense for the Holy Place. According to all that I have commanded you, they shall do."[6] (emphasis added)

This passage is about the instructions to make the things for the tabernacle and later the temple in Jerusalem and who would do the work. We see that the Lord has gifted certain men, by name, with the skills, knowledge, and intellect to perform these duties. The expectation is that these men would put their skills and knowledge to work for the one public project Israel had at the time, but the skills were given to these men and no restrictions were placed on them for using those skills in whatever other ways they chose; these skills and knowledge were now their property.

This passage establishes, or reiterates and defines, the property justice system. This is discussed in much more detail in the next chapter but it is important that processes, penalties, and punishments are not arbitrary but fully established and applicable to all regardless of position or place in society.

As an aside, it can also be pointed out that this passage speaks to a fundamental concept of economic growth that descends from defined property rights, division of labor. This great insight from Adam Smith is evident throughout the Bible from Cain (farmer) and Abel (herdsman) to Genesis 4, where some early tribes are listed and identified by their skills and specializations. Later (1 Kings 6), Solomon is contracting for skilled labor to build the temple, and in the New Testament Peter was a fisherman (Matthew 4) as were several other apostles, Paul was a tentmaker (Acts 18), Lydia was a merchant in high end fabrics (Acts 16), and of course Jesus was a carpenter/stone worker/craftsman (Mark 6). Specialization and division of labor are important to growth and prosperity and Deuteronomy laid a foundation where this sort of economic arrangement could emerge allowing numerous cities to develop, some which still stand to this day (Jerusalem being most prominent and important but not the only one) and marketplaces to develop as well as international trade.

These passages, and others not mentioned here, make it clear that property rights and protections do not apply to just land and animals. Since Israel, like almost all ancient societies, was agrarian, animals and land were certainly the most plentiful, obvious, and important examples, but certainly not the only kinds of property.

The broader definition of property is also found in the commandment to not covet. First introduced with the other Ten Commandments in Exodus 20, it is restated in Deuteronomy 5: "[A]nd you shall not covet your neighbor's wife. And you shall not desire your neighbor's house, his field, or his male servant, or his female servant, his ox, or his donkey, or anything that is your neighbor's."[7] This is a list that runs the range of items from that which is your neighbor through relationships to those in his care to actual tangible property to "anything that is your neighbor's." Coveting is the only mental commandment. While Jesus would later explain that violating commandments as a sin starts with a thought or an attitude. The violation as a crime required an action: murder, theft, adultery, lying, worshiping idols, or an omission like forgetting the Sabbath or ignoring one's parents. Coveting is the only one that was always clearly understood as a mental act and it dealt with property. While all the things listed in the passage are tangible, if the sin can be intangible then so can the object of the sin.

Property rights are also implied in numerous other places. Deuteronomy 15 is one of several passages where the people are told to be generous:

> At the end of every seven years you shall grant a remission of debts. This is the manner of remission: every creditor shall release what he has loaned to his neighbor; he shall not exact it of his neighbor and his brother, because the LORD's remission has been proclaimed. From a foreigner you may exact it, but your hand shall release whatever of yours is with your brother. . . . If there is a poor man with you, one of your brothers, in any of your towns in your land . . . you shall not harden your heart, nor close your hand from your poor brother; but you shall freely open your hand to him, and shall generously lend him sufficient for his need in whatever he lacks. . . . You shall freely open your hand to your brother, to your needy and poor in your land.[8]

There is something to be said about capital formation and capital markets in this passage, but the focus here is property. One cannot lend or forgive loans if one does not own the property to begin with and still have a claim on it. The language is clear: "whatever is yours," "generously lend," and "what he has loaned" clearly indicates that people own property and while they were expected to be generous and helpful to the needy, the property was theirs to do with as they wanted. It is important to note that just a few verses before these, in the same chapter, it is asserted that if the people just follow the rules set forth in this book, there will be no poor and needy: "there will be no poor among you; for the Lord will bless you in the land that the Lord your God is giving you for an inheritance to possess—if only you will strictly obey the voice of the Lord your God, being careful to do all this commandment that I command you today."[9] This verse has spiritual implications as most verses do but it also has tangible temporal application. Within the context of the chapter, it is talking about material prosperity; lending, charity, and household and farm management are the other subjects in this chapter. In many ways this is the heart of Deuteronomy which lays out all the necessary conditions for prosperity with private property being foundational. Taking care of one's family, being generous and charitable, giving tithes and offering to God, and so forth all start with people owning things and having a right to use them as they see fit. Being generous makes no sense in the absence of private property, one cannot be generous with community property or other people's property. Generosity implies choice and sacrifice, and neither of these apply without private property. People choose what to do with their property and the choices they make exhibit their heart and spiritual condition but have real tangible effects on material prosperity and economic growth. But it is clear that private property is foundational for an economy to flourish.

## NOT JUST FOR MEN

Another important aspect besides the broad definition of property is the wider definition of property owner. While Christian nations restricted property ownership by race, gender, class, and religion at different times throughout their history, we do not actually see such restrictions in the Bible itself. We see a court case settled by the Lord Himself through Moses that set a universal precedent on property inheritance and ownership:

> Then drew near the daughters of Zelophehad the son of Hepher, son of Gilead, son of Machir, son of Manasseh, from the clans of Manasseh the son of Joseph. The names of his daughters were: Mahlah, Noah, Hoglah, Milcah, and Tirzah. And they stood before Moses and before Eleazar the priest and before the chiefs and all the congregation, at the entrance of the tent of meeting, saying, "Our father died in the wilderness. He was not among the company of those who gathered themselves together against the Lord in the company of Korah, but died for his own sin. And he had no sons. Why should the name of our father be taken away from his clan because he had no son? Give to us a possession among our father's brothers." Moses brought their case before the Lord. And the Lord said to Moses, "The daughters of Zelophehad are right. You shall give them possession of an inheritance among their father's brothers and transfer the inheritance of their father to them. And you shall speak to the people of Israel, saying, 'If a man dies and has no son, then you shall transfer his inheritance to his daughter.'"[10]

In other passages we see single mothers owning land and earning income from it (2 Kings 8), and Proverbs 31, a passage I will return to later, talks of a woman engaging in a variety of economic activities including considering a field and buying it and investing her own earnings (verse 16).

In addition to women, we know that Israelites were commanded to treat non-Jews who lived among them as equals and in the previous discussion about human rights and the rights of aliens, we saw that some aliens were included in the initial inheritance.

The Promised Land was just that: land. It was property that had to be tended and worked to be productive, which meant using certain kinds of small property like tools and animals combined with skills and hard work to grow the crops needed for consumption and the marketplace. God protected all that property with strong laws and significant penalties, He clearly defined property broadly and did not exclude anyone from being a property owner. His only caveat was the reminder that the earth is His and all that is in it and everyone is ultimately a lease holder and not a true owner.

## THE EARLY CHURCH AND SOCIALISM

But what about the early church? We live in the church age now and some of those laws in Deuteronomy no longer apply, such as the dietary laws which were explicitly addressed in the New Testament (Mark 7, Acts 10). Along that same thinking, the early church lived in a communal setting as described in Acts 4:

> Now the full number of those who believed were of one heart and soul, and no one said that any of the things that belonged to him was his own, but they had everything in common. And with great power the apostles were giving their testimony to the resurrection of the Lord Jesus, and great grace was upon them all. There was not a needy person among them, for as many as were owners of lands or houses sold them and brought the proceeds of what was sold and laid it at the apostles' feet, and it was distributed to each as any had need. Thus Joseph, who was also called by the apostles Barnabas (which means son of encouragement), a Levite, a native of Cyprus, sold a field that belonged to him and brought the money and laid it at the apostles' feet.[11]

This passage has been used by many to assert that the New Testament church is to be more collectivist, to forge a sharing economy. After all, no less of a figure than Karl Marx argued that society goes through economic stages and that there is a stage for a nation to have private property and market-based economic activity but that mature and progressing societies grow past that stage eventually and enter into a more communal arrangement with socialism leading to pure communism. Is that not what we are seeing here as we look across 1,500 years of biblical history? Did God's economy start out as a property-based market system and with enlightenment did it mature into a collectivist system? There are political movements, theologians, and other academics, both historically and currently, that look to the scriptures, and these verses in particular, for their claim that the Bible supports a socialist economic structure. They also look at certain passages in the minor prophets where the wealthy are condemned for being abusive, greedy, and unjust as further support for their claim. There is another group that does not go as far as to say the Bible is socialist but does claim it is neutral on the issues of property and economic organizational structure. Since so much of this claim hangs on the attitude and disposition of private property, it seems appropriate to address it.

## PROPERTY AND THE EARLY CHURCH

The passages from Acts 4 quoted above have some very powerful phrases in them; "no one said that any of the things belonged to him was his own" and "they had everything in common." This would seemingly give strong support for a collectivist system but there are extenuating factors to consider.

There is no indication that this was an economic arrangement for outside of the church. This passage is clear that it only applied within the church and later context implies that it only applied to the early church. The faithful sold their lands and houses and fields presumably in the larger marketplace and donated the funds to the church, who then used the funds to help those in need. There is no indication that this model was meant for a larger polity such as a nation, a region, or even a village or town. This model worked under these unique circumstances at that time for reasons that are very hard to replicate in a larger community. The church was relatively small and so there was a high degree of personal knowledge between the members.

It was a close-knit community and they were together every day. The church was small, which certainly helped with addressing the knowledge issue, and it was under various levels of persecution which tends to bring the persecuted closer together. However, we do not see this same model once the church grows and has multiple locations. We do see churches helping each other financially but there is no indication that there was ever a full-blown communal church sub-economy. Indeed, there are references to members owning homes and other forms of property throughout the New Testament. It is clear that communal living was not a model that was exported to other churches, let alone expected of a larger community.

Within the context of these verses in Acts there is indication that even this first church in Jerusalem was not living in as a communal arrangement as some assume. In chapter 4, quoted above, we are told that Barnabas sold *a* field. We want to be careful about reading too much into translated verses, there can be room for other interpretations especially of a small word that may seem incidental. The above excerpt is from the English Standard Version (ESV), the version I use for all verses in this book, but here are some other translations:

Having land, sold it (King James)
and who owned a tract of land, sold it and (NASB)
having a field, sold it, (ASV)
Having a field, got money for it (Basic English Bible)
He sold a field that belonged to him (NSRV)

Of the most common English translations, all but one translates this verse as Barnabas having had *a* piece of property that he sold and none imply or state that he sold *all* he had. This is a critical point in that the early church was not living in a communal arrangement as pioneers of a new economy but were providing financial support to the church.

Furthermore, in Acts 5 we see the incident with Ananias and Sapphira, who were struck dead over selling property, so some conclude. That conclusion stretches the text and a careful reading shows that they were not struck dead for greed or clinging to their property, Peter actually defends private property in this verse:

> But a man named Ananias, with his wife Sapphira, sold a piece of property, and with his wife's knowledge he kept back for himself some of the proceeds and brought only a part of it and laid it at the apostles' feet. But Peter said, "Ananias, why has Satan filled your heart to lie to the Holy Spirit and to keep back for yourself part of the proceeds of the land? While it remained unsold, did it not remain your own? And after it was sold, was it not at your disposal? Why is it that you have contrived this deed in your heart? You have not lied to man but to God." When Ananias heard these words, he fell down and breathed his last. And great fear came upon all who heard of it. The young men rose and wrapped him up and carried him out and buried him.
>
> After an interval of about three hours his wife came in, not knowing what had happened. And Peter said to her, "Tell me whether you sold the land for so much." And she said, "Yes, for so much." But Peter said to her, "How is it that you have agreed together to test the Spirit of the Lord? Behold, the feet of those who have buried your husband are at the door, and they will carry you out." Immediately she fell down at his feet and breathed her last. When the young men came in they found her dead, and they carried her out and buried her beside her husband. And great fear came upon the whole church and upon all who heard of these things.[12]

Peter condemned both of them for lying to the Holy Spirit, the lie happened to be about property and money, but Peter is clear that the land was Ananias's to do with as he saw fit, and the proceeds from the sale were Ananias's as well to do with as he saw fit. What happened was Ananias claimed one thing and did another, the property was incidental to the overall situation. His wife was no less culpable and this implies equal responsibility and equal stake in the property, it was Sapphira's to do with as she saw fit as well, but also hers was to pay the full price for their sin as well. So even in a sin that deals with property Peter defends the right to property and the right to manage one's property as one sees fit. He did not exert a claim on the property for the church in any way and there was no assumption of communal ownership until after a pledge had been made by the owners.

## JUBILEE

Another passage some point to comes from the Old Testament, and that is the passages dealing with Jubilee.

> You shall count seven weeks of years, seven times seven years, so that the time of the seven weeks of years shall give you forty-nine years. Then you shall sound the loud trumpet on the tenth day of the seventh month. On the Day of Atonement you shall sound the trumpet throughout all your land. And you shall consecrate the fiftieth year, and proclaim liberty throughout the land to all its inhabitants. It shall be a jubilee for you, when each of you shall return to his property and each of you shall return to his clan. That fiftieth year shall be a jubilee for you; in it you shall neither sow nor reap what grows of itself nor gather the grapes from the undressed vines. For it is a jubilee. It shall be holy to you. You may eat the produce of the field.
>
> In this year of jubilee each of you shall return to his property. And if you make a sale to your neighbor or buy from your neighbor, you shall not wrong one another. You shall pay your neighbor according to the number of years after the jubilee, and he shall sell to you according to the number of years for crops. If the years are many, you shall increase the price, and if the years are few, you shall reduce the price, for it is the number of the crops that he is selling to you.[13]

Some see this as a early redistribution plan in which the land primarily but other property as well would be transferred from the wealthy to the poor. There may be some truth to this since this required all the land in the nation to be returned to the original family that owned it. However, the verse itself addresses larger misconception.

First, it is true that this is a plan to make sure that over the long term, land, property, and certain other property reverted back to its original owner, but this was not a scheme for communal ownership nor was it a plan that actually prevented the market system from working or significantly inhibited wealth creation in favor of equality. The passage itself makes it clear that prices of property are actually leases that expire in the Jubilee year and that property could be transferred and used for productive purposes and what was produced from it belonged to the leaser.

Second, it is widely concluded that Jubilee was not about redistribution but "there is significant consensus among biblical scholars that Jubilee actually entailed the completed payment of a debt, not its forgiveness."[14]

Third, this is one of those commands that seems to stand in both the spiritual and economic camp. It is tied to the Day of Atonement and the year is to be thought of as holy. While honesty, fairness, and charity are traits we should encourage and are essential to a well-functioning economy and society, Jubilee, as described in Leviticus, is not redistributionist but also is not a principle which a modern secular society would incorporate.

## SUMMARY

The Bible is clear that private property is an essential part of the way God organized an economy that could flourish. There is no example of widespread wealth or property redistribution although private charity was expected. Furthermore, the biblical discussion of property reinforces the naturalness of it, the Bible does not have to define private property or establish it an institution, it just starts off protecting its practice and that is what any society that wants to flourish will also do.

## NOTES

1. *Genesis*, n.d., 15:1–20.
2. Craig L. Blomberg, "Neither Capitalism nor Socialism: A Biblical Theology of Economics," *Journal of Markets and Morality* 15, no. 1 (Spring 2012): 209, https://www.marketsandmorality.com/index.php/mandm/article/viewFile/705/685.
3. *Deuteronomy*, n.d., 19:14 (ESV).
4. *Exodus*, n.d., 22:1–14 (ESV).
5. Deuteronomy 24:14–15
6. *Exodus*, 31:1–11 (ESV).
7. Deuteronomy 5:21
8. *Deuteronomy*, 15:1–15 (Selected) (ESV).
9. Ibid., 15:5–6 (ESV).
10. *Numbers*, n.d., 26:1–8 (ESV).
11. *Acts of the Apostles*, n.d., 4:32–35 (ESV).
12. Ibid., 5:1–10 (ESV).
13. *Leviticus*, n.d., 25:8–16.
14. Arthur Lindsley, ed., *Counting the Cost: Christian Perspectives on Capitalism* (Abilene: Abilene Christian University Press, 2017), 71.

## *Chapter Five*

# Thou Shall Not Bear False Witness

## *The Legal and Regulatory System*

There are at least two ways to look at any social institution: at its specific actions and results and at its institutional design. Specific actions tend to be more obvious and easier to analyze; law that prohibits women from driving is obvious and has certain costs and benefits (to some I suppose) that can be evaluated. The institutional design—how laws are made, changed, and enforced—is less obvious. They are harder to see and harder to analyze, but that does not mean they should be ignored. I have discussed a variety of specific elements of the Deuteronomic legal system in other chapters, the purpose of this chapter is to discuss the institutional design of the Deuteronomic legal system, not specific laws like prohibition on theft or murder, but to discuss the principles of a good set of laws. The question that this chapter seeks to answer is, how is a proper justice system structured?

There is, of course, one glaring exception of the ancient Israel legal code compared to any other, it is widely accepted by billions through the years to have come directly from God. Obviously no modern set of laws makes such a claim but that does not really impact the overall application to modern society. It may surprise those who are not well versed in the Old Testament that the first condition of a good set of laws is the consent of the people.

### PEOPLE'S CONSENT

A few months after the Israelites fled Egypt, they set up camp at the base of Mount Sinai, or, as some versions put it, near a mountain in the wilderness of Sinai. Moses ascended the mountain and then descended to deliver a message from God, which was in the form of a proposal (indeed some scholars and the

Bible itself point out the very interesting parallels between the Sinai experience and a Jewish wedding ceremony, see Jeremiah 31:32):

> "Thus you shall say to the house of Jacob, and tell the people of Israel: 'You yourselves have seen what I did to the Egyptians, and how I bore you on eagles' wings and brought you to myself. Now therefore, if you will indeed obey my voice and keep my covenant, you shall be my treasured possession among all peoples, for all the earth is mine; and you shall be to me a kingdom of priests and a holy nation.' These are the words that you shall speak to the people of Israel." So Moses came and called the elders of the people and set before them all these words that the Lord had commanded him. All the people answered together and said, "All that the Lord has spoken we will do." And Moses reported the words of the people to the Lord.[1]

Before the laws were ever offered, Moses climbed the mountain so he could deliver that simple proposal to the emerging Jewish nation to which they agreed. Presumably they could have declined—we have no idea what that would have meant and looked like, there is nothing in the passage that indicates there was punishment for a wrong decision so we cannot know. But God was not forcing himself but offering himself to the people and desired their consent. This is not the only time either.

After the conquest of the Promised Land, Joshua, who assumed leadership after Moses died, and was one of the two oldest people in the nation, put the choice before the new generation of Israelites:

> "Now fear the LORD and serve him with all faithfulness. Throw away the gods your ancestors worshiped beyond the Euphrates River and in Egypt, and serve the LORD. But if serving the LORD seems undesirable to you, then choose for yourselves this day whom you will serve, whether the gods your ancestors served beyond the Euphrates, or the gods of the Amorites, in whose land you are living. But as for me and my household, we will serve the LORD."
>
> Then the people answered, "Far be it from us to forsake the LORD to serve other gods! It was the LORD our God himself who brought us and our parents up out of Egypt, from that land of slavery, and performed those great signs before our eyes. He protected us on our entire journey and among all the nations through which we traveled. And the LORD drove out before us all the nations, including the Amorites, who lived in the land. We too will serve the LORD, because he is our God."
>
> Joshua said to the people, "You are not able to serve the LORD. He is a holy God; he is a jealous God. He will not forgive your rebellion and your sins. If you forsake the LORD and serve foreign gods, he will turn and bring disaster on you and make an end of you, after he has been good to you."
>
> But the people said to Joshua, "No! We will serve the LORD."

> Then Joshua said, "You are witnesses against yourselves that you have chosen to serve the LORD."
>
> "Yes, we are witnesses," they replied.
>
> "Now then," said Joshua, "throw away the foreign gods that are among you and yield your hearts to the LORD, the God of Israel."
>
> And the people said to Joshua, "We will serve the LORD our God and obey him."[2]

There is much for the theologians to discuss and debate in this passage but Joshua, the political and military leader of the nation, asked the people whom they wanted to follow, which implies whose rules and laws and so forth the nation would follow, and the people's consent was once again solicited.

So one biblical characteristic of a good justice system is that the people consent to the laws under which they live. Laws can come from several sources: political leaders can impose or propose them or laws can emerge from common practice or they can be some hybrid. But ultimately all laws need to meet the standard that they have been approved by the people who have to live under them. This consent can take different forms from the whole nation expressing its preference in a pure democracy to representatives speaking for the people but the point is that consent by the people of the laws under which they must live is a first principle of a proper justice system.

## CLEAR AND KNOWN

Another first principle is that the laws must be understandable and known to all, or at least available to all. Before the people consented to the law Moses delivered to Israel, he read the law to them. Even before the Ten Commandments were issued, Moses was teaching the people the laws so they would know:

> Moses' father-in-law said to him, "What you are doing is not good. You and the people with you will certainly wear yourselves out, for the thing is too heavy for you. You are not able to do it alone. Now obey my voice; I will give you advice, and God be with you! You shall represent the people before God and bring their cases to God, and you shall warn them about the statutes and the laws, and make them know the way in which they must walk and what they must do. . . ." So Moses listened to the voice of his father-in-law and did all that he had said.[3]

In Exodus 20 God speaks the Ten Commandments to all the people; "And God spoke all these words, saying . . ."[4] but the people were afraid and asked that Moses alone speak with God and that Moses tell them what God had said. "Now when all the people saw the thunder and the flashes of lightning and the sound of the trumpet and the mountain smoking, the people were afraid and trembled, and they stood far off and said to Moses, 'You speak to us, and we will listen; but do not let God speak to us, lest we die.'"[5] A few verses later we read, "And the LORD said to Moses, Thus you shall say to the people of Israel,"[6] and then the next three chapters are the details of the laws that God had given Moses.

If we fast-forward a few decades to Deuteronomy we see the same themes. Essentially the entire book is a telling and explaining of a number of things, history and theology but also of the laws God had given. The book's name means a retelling of the law and the book opens with "And the LORD said to Moses, 'Thus you shall say to the people of Israel:'"[7] and then there are thirty-two chapters of content the people needed to know about who God is, who they were, and how they were supposed to live, the bulk of which were social laws. In chapter 4 we read, "And now, O Israel, listen to the statutes and the rules that I am teaching you,"[8] and chapter 5 starts, "And Moses summoned all Israel and said to them, 'Hear, O Israel, the statutes and the rules that I speak in your hearing today, and you shall learn them and be careful to do them.'"[9]

While it seems pretty clear that Moses wanted the nation of Israel to know the law, it was also to be intergenerational. In chapter 6 Moses makes it clear each generation has a duty and responsibility to teach the new generation and to keep these laws ever present:

> Now this is the commandment—the statutes and the rules—that the LORD your God commanded me to teach you, that you may do them in the land to which you are going over, to possess it, that you may fear the LORD your God, you and your son and your son's son, by keeping all his statutes and his commandments, which I command you, all the days of your life, and that your days may be long. Hear therefore, O Israel, and be careful to do them, that it may go well with you, and that you may multiply greatly, as the LORD, the God of your fathers, has promised you, in a land flowing with milk and honey.
>
> Hear, O Israel: The LORD our God, the LORD is one. You shall love the LORD your God with all your heart and with all your soul and with all your might. And these words that I command you today shall be on your heart. You shall teach them diligently to your children, and shall talk of them when you sit in your house, and when you walk by the way, and when you lie down, and when you rise. You shall bind them as a sign on your hand, and they shall be as frontlets between your eyes. You shall write them on the doorposts of your house and on your gates.[10]

Everyone was to know the law, be taught the law, and then become a teacher of the law. They were to have the law written in obvious places where they would see it and even carry some of it with them at all times. There were theological and spiritual implications to all of this but the rules and what is to be taught is not restricted, laws protecting property and dealing with human rights and so forth are all part of this mixture of "the statute and the rules" that was going make the days of their life be long and prosperous.

One reason that everyone was to know the law is that it is easy to drift from the law over time. Convenience, political expediency, desire to do something else can all cause nations to ignore their laws. Some may see a constitution as a hindrance to "getting things done." Israel lost the book of Deuteronomy at one point. We are not sure how long it was missing but it was found and they realized how far they had drifted from their founding document. King Josiah was reigning when Deuteronomy was rediscovered, the full story starts in 2 Kings 22, and the first thing he did was inquire if this was truly God's covenant with Israel, interestingly enough it was a woman prophet named Huldah that confirmed it, and "then the king called together all the elders of Judah and Jerusalem. He went up to the temple of the LORD with the people of Judah, the inhabitants of Jerusalem, the priests and the prophets—all the people from the least to the greatest. He read in their hearing all the words of the Book of the Covenant, which had been found in the temple of the LORD."[11] This led to a significant number of reforms and changes in Israel. This episode warns us as to how easy it is to lose freedom, the natural drift of human history is toward tyranny; Greek democracy did not last, Rome went from republic to empire, many nations have never experienced anything resembling freedom, and even the nation of Israel, whose very existence, not just political identity, was tied to 'keeping the law' lost it. Literally, lost it. Laws need to be well known and clearly understood and this applies from generation to generation or any emergency, charismatic strongman, or apathetic people can lose them.

Now, I should note, that this is not to argue that just because a law is old it should be maintained, or that a change to bad laws is to be avoided. But that is not the concern. More often than not the powerful turn the law into a weapon to maintain power and enrich themselves, which brings me to the next principle.

## UNBIASED AND EVENLY APPLIED

Maybe the most important aspect of a legal system is that it applies to everyone equally, even a system with bad laws is better if everyone must live under the same bad laws, they are far more likely to get changed if they are evenly applied. The politically powerful and connected should live under the same laws that everyone else lives under. In much of the world people live under a two-tiered legal system that works well for the powerful and not so well or can even be a hindrance to most of the population. This was a problem in biblical times and remains a problem in many nations today. And this is not just a problem with overtly corrupt politics, even in advanced countries we see laws passed from which the legislature will exempt themselves. In the United States, members of Congress are exempt from everything from speeding tickets (when on the way to a Congressional session) to insider trading on stock information.

Leviticus may make the most succinct and firm statement on the issue. In a large passage dealing with how to properly live in a community there is this instruction: "You shall do no injustice in court. You shall not be partial to the poor or defer to the great, but in righteousness shall you judge your neighbor. You shall not go around as a slanderer among your people, and you shall not stand up against the life of your neighbor: I am the LORD."[12] Justice is to be equally applied with no regard to the position of status or the people involved. We see this restated in Deuteronomy 16 but extended to specifically include judges and ties this command directly to the nation's prosperity: "You shall appoint judges and officers in all your towns that the LORD your God is giving you, according to your tribes, and they shall judge the people with righteous judgment. You shall not pervert justice. You shall not show partiality, and you shall not accept a bribe, for a bribe blinds the eyes of the wise and subverts the cause of the righteous. Justice, and only justice, you shall follow, that you may live and inherit the land that the LORD your God is giving you."[13] Beyond the actual corruption, subverting justice can cause a loss of confidence in the legal system. Such a loss, if widespread enough, can bring an economy to a grinding halt as people do not trust courts to enforce contracts or protect private property or possibly even punish criminals. Unfortunately for Israel the temptation then as now is for those with power to pervert the law and turn it into a weapon to benefit themselves, often at the expense of others.

The prophet Amos in his poetic lament for Israel in chapter 5 cites the abuse of justice as one of the many actions leading to Israel's coming problems:

> They hate him who reproves in the gate,
> and they abhor him who speaks the truth.
> Therefore because you trample on the poor
> and you exact taxes of grain from him,
> you have built houses of hewn stone,
> but you shall not dwell in them;
> you have planted pleasant vineyards,
> but you shall not drink their wine.
> For I know how many are your transgressions
> and how great are your sins—
> you who afflict the righteous, who take a bribe,
> and turn aside the needy in the gate.

> Therefore he who is prudent will keep silent in such a time,
> for it is an evil time.
> Seek good, and not evil,
> that you may live;
> and so the LORD, the God of hosts, will be with you,
> as you have said.
> Hate evil, and love good,
> and establish justice in the gate;
> it may be that the LORD, the God of hosts,
> will be gracious to the remnant of Joseph.[14]

Amos points out that the tax system was weaponized to oppress the poor and fund an extravagant lifestyle by the leaders and judges who were taking bribes.

While about one hundred years after, King Ahab and his wife, Jezebel, provide a perfect example of the sort of perversion to which Amos was referring. King Ahab wanted to purchase a vineyard from a man named Naboth but Naboth would not sell, which shows that even in the most corrupt times, property rights were still respected. So, Ahab and mostly his wife, Queen Jezebel, hatched a plan:

> So she [Jezebel] wrote letters in Ahab's name and sealed them with his seal, and she sent the letters to the elders and the leaders who lived with Naboth in his city. And she wrote in the letters, "Proclaim a fast, and set Naboth at the head of the people. And set two worthless men opposite him, and let them bring a charge against him, saying, 'You have cursed God and the king.' Then take him out and stone him to death." And the men of his city, the elders and the leaders who lived in his city, did as Jezebel had sent word to them. As it was written in the letters that she had sent to them, they proclaimed a fast and set Naboth at the head of the people. And the two worthless men came in and sat opposite him. And the worthless men brought a charge against Naboth in the presence of the people, saying, "Naboth cursed God and the king." So they took him outside the city and stoned him to death with stones. Then they sent to Jezebel, saying, "Naboth has been stoned; he is dead." As soon as Jezebel heard that Naboth had been stoned and was dead, Jezebel said to Ahab, "Arise, take possession of the vineyard of Naboth the Jezreelite, which he refused to give you for money, for Naboth is not alive, but dead."[15]

The king and queen as well as the local leaders all conspired to kill Naboth just so Ahab could have a vineyard and stop throwing a tantrum. They are obviously corrupt in many ways and one way was a subversion of the legal system to have an innocent man executed.

Meanwhile, King David, about three hundred years before Ahab, provides an example of how power can corrupt even the best of leaders, but also how the law should be applied. After David's adultery with Bathsheba and ultimate betrayal and death of her soldier husband, the prophet Nathan confronted David with a fake legal matter that paralleled David's actions. David does not recognize the similarities between Nathan's case and David's own actions and prescribes a proper punishment for the offender in Nathan's story. Then Nathan reveals that David is the offender in his story and David realizes the weight and magnitude of his crime and willingly accepts his punishment, which was severe.

## Modern Versions of Legal Bias

While the killing of opponents and critics and others that irritate the powerful has not stopped, we tend to see modern corruption and legal system perversions in different ways today. One significant way that impacts economic development is the difference in how long it takes to start a business depending on the applicant's income level, which is just a proxy measure for connections and social capital. As reported by the World Bank a high-income applicant can get a business started relatively quickly. This may not seem like a significant issue but it indicates two important points: 1) many countries have two legal systems, one for the rich and powerful and one for everyone else, and 2) there is a bias in favor of some and against others which means that for some people, their ideas and possible production are not valued.

The good news is that most countries have moved toward getting businesses started faster even in the just the past few years, but the bad news is there is still a significant distinction between how fast wealthy regions enable a business and how fast poor ones do. This is more about overall efficiency and different attitudes toward commerce between countries, which is a cultural issue I return to in a later chapter. But there is also a distinction between how fast the wealthy and the poor within a country can get a business started, especially in the developing world.

The World Bank table from which Table 2.5.1 is an excerpt covers almost every country in the world and the very good news is that in the last fourteen years the world average to start a business has gone from 51 days to 20 days. That is unimaginable progress when we think about how many nations had to improve to shrink the global average that much. There are remarkable changes like Azerbaijan going from 105 days to 5 days and even improvements in developed nations like Austria going from 25 days to 21 but even in this overall good news, some are going backward like Cambodia going from 95 to 99 days, that is not much but when it already takes over three months it is an unfortunate development that is fixable. The leaders in this measure are New Zealand, 1 day; Hong Kong, 2 days; and Singapore, 3 days. The losers are Venezuela, 230 days; the aforementioned Cambodia; and Haiti, 97 days (and this was a big improvement over

**Table 2.5.1. Days to Start a Business Around the World**[1]

| *Region* | *Days to Start a Business (2017)* |
|---|---|
| Arab World | 22 |
| East Asia and Pacific | 20 |
| East Asia and Pacific (excluding high income) | 26 |
| Europe & Central Asia | 10 |
| Europe & Central Asia (excluding high income) | 11 |
| Latin America & Caribbean | 31 |
| Latin America & Caribbean (excluding high income) | 39 |
| Middle East & North Africa | 19 |
| Middle East & North Africa (excluding high income) | 21 |
| North America | 4 |
| Sub-Saharan Africa | 24 |
| Sub-Saharan Africa (excluding high income) | 24 |
| Sub-Sahara (high income) | 11 |
| Sub-Saharan Africa (low income) | 24 |

1. "Time Required to Start a Business (Days)" (The World Bank, n.d.), https://data.worldbank.org/indicator/IC.REG.DURS?view=chart.

the 260 days in 2003). We must also remember these are national averages and there may be large regional differences within a country as the data shows there are between income groups.

From the data in Table 2.5.1, it takes a little over 24 days for a non-wealthy person to start a business in the regions dominated by developing nations. When including the wealthy that number falls to 18 days, it shaves a week off the average for the entire population which means the wealthy are actually getting their businesses started much faster. There are fewer wealthy and to reduce the average by a week means they are getting their businesses started in just a few days or less.

Some may point out that the wealthy have better connections and can hire legal talent to get quickly through the licensing and permitting process and so it is fully expected that they would be able to start a business in a shorter amount of time, but that *is* the issue. Laws should not be designed and enforced in such a way that the wealthy and connected have an advantage. Hiring legal talent and having political connections should not be needed to get a permit to open a business and when such measures are needed it lowers growth by preventing ideas from becoming reality and causing people to divert resources to red-tape navigators and not into investment and hiring. The sad truth is that some laws are designed to be weapons against the poor and favor the connected but the reality is any law can be a weapon, if misused or in the wrong hands, and all of that legal gymnastics comes at a high price.

## NOT MANY

There is a temptation to think that every incident and possible scenario needs a law to address it. The phrase 'there ought to be a law!', sometimes said in jest and sometimes serious, is common. Whenever a high-profile incident occurs, something that makes the papers and television and internet, people soon emerge calling for more regulations and new laws to ensure it does not happen again, as though some words on a piece of paper can stop all bad people from acting and prevent bad things from happening. Contrary to this desire and perceived need that the legal system must be dynamic and constantly evolving to address the changing society, the Bible establishes a set of laws, around 600, of which about 400 dealt with worship, the temple/tabernacle, the sacrifice system, dietary restrictions, and so forth, leaving a little over 200 that actually dealt with living as a community.[16] Furthermore there is no mechanism for changing them or adding to them. All 613 are summed up in the Ten Commandments and later, Christ sums them up in two commandments which can effectively be boiled down to six words: love God and love your neighbor.

I do not want to apply a principle where one does not exist. There is nothing superior about having 613 laws and there are certainly reasons to change laws from time to time and even make new ones. But the clear principle in both the Old Testament and New is that many laws and a growing body of laws is oppressive. As Jesus observed about the Pharisees:

> Then Jesus said to the crowds and to his disciples, "The scribes and the Pharisees sit on Moses' seat, so do and observe whatever they tell you, but not the works they do. For they preach, but do not practice. They tie up heavy burdens, hard to bear, and lay them on people's shoulders, but they themselves are not willing to move them with their finger."[17]

There are several points here, but the Pharisees laid burdens on people in how they explained the law should be applied and followed, they weaponized the law and they did not live under the same laws they required of others, and they made many laws beyond what was in the Bible.

## SUMMARY

People are flawed and prone to sin. Giving such a creature power over others is an invitation to corruption and abuses, as Lord Acton years ago quipped: power corrupts. But there must be a legal system and it must be enforced. How does a community empower some people called the government to enforce laws necessary to a well-functioning society but keep those same people from becoming the biggest threat to society by misusing their power? The Bible gives us some basic principles on how to balance these two opposing needs and what a functioning proper legal system looks like. It is not really a secret formula but it does seem difficult. Israel actually physically lost its law book, its constitution, for a long enough period of time that once it was found again many, many reforms had to be undertaken to get back into compliance. We do not know how long it was missing but it only takes a generation or two to lose freedom and along with it, prosperity. Overall, the process is simple; the people should consent to the laws under which they will live, the laws need to be applied equally to all, the laws should be clear and easily understood, and there should not be an overabundance of them. Any government that deviates from these principles, even if they feel it is for good reasons, is violating a fundamental governing principle and risks becoming oppressive.

## NOTES

1. *Exodus*, n.d., 19:3–8 (ESV).
2. *Joshua*, n.d., 24:14–24 (ESV).
3. *Exodus*, 17:17–20, 24 (ESV).
4. Ibid., 20:1 (ESV).
5. Ibid., 20:8–9 (ESV).
6. Exodus 20:22 ESV
7. *Deuteronomy*, n.d., 1:1 (ESV).
8. Ibid., 4:1 (ESV).
9. Ibid., 5:1 (ESV).
10. Ibid., 6:1–9 (ESV).
11. *2 Kings*, n.d., 22:1–2 (ESV).
12. *Leviticus*, n.d., 19:15–16 (ESV).
13. *Deuteronomy*, 16:18–20 (ESV).
14. *Amos*, n.d., 5:10–15 (ESV).
15. *1 Kings*, n.d., 21:8–14.
16. "The Law: All 613 Commandments!," accessed July 12, 2018, https://www.gospeloutreach.net/613laws.html.
17. *Matthew*, n.d., 23:1–3 (ESV).

*Chapter Six*

# The Biblical Role for Civil Government

The role of government in development and generating economic prosperity is controversial to say the least. The prevailing approach over the last fifty to sixty years has been that development needed to be led by national governments. This has been the underlying intellectual foundation that has supported many of the efforts by the United Nations, the International Monetary Fund, and the World Bank as well as individual wealthy nations. Much of what these institutions has done is transfer resources to the governments of the poor nations in hopes that the resources will be used to create economic opportunities and jump-start the growth process. Decades of experience have shown us that this is not effective, at least not as effective as advertised and hoped. Despite these results and strong arguments from Western critics like William Easterly, Theodore Dalrymple, and the Acton Institute and African critics like Paul Kagame, George Ayittey, and Dambisa Moyo, there are many prominent people like Bill Gates, Jeffrey Sachs, and the various international institutions in the aid industry who adhere to the aid approach.

The question that must be asked, in light of the less than hoped for and often very disappointing results is, why did this process get started and why do people still adhere to it? Determining how it got started is a little nebulous, who can say for sure when a process such as this had a start date? But one significant encouragement in pursuing this activist government path was the Marshall Plan. Officially known as the European Recovery Plan, the Marshall Plan was the brainchild of American secretary of state General George Marshall and his staff and was the American plan to help rebuild Europe in the wake of World War II. It was a four-year plan that largely involved transferring large sums of money ($13 billion in 1948 dollars, over $100 billion in current dollars) over a four-year period from the United States to the eighteen

Western European national governments, the countries within the Soviet sphere of influence declined to participate.

Although there is significant debate in some circles today, the Marshall Plan was credited with Western Europe's recovery from the war, Marshall was awarded the Nobel Peace Prize (the only person to win it while currently serving in a military) and lauded and feted in several European countries in the following years. This success provided a blueprint, rightly or wrongly, for helping other struggling economies. This has proven a mixed bag at best.

Before I go any further, I want to be clear; aid has had positive impact at times and in places. It can be argued over whether it was the best use of funds and the most effective programs, those are useful discussions that need to be held, but aid has its place especially in the wake of disasters, whether natural or manmade, where people have immediate needs. In these cases, the delivery of resources to alleviate suffering and save lives is absolutely the right response and should be supported. However, this is not the model for long-term development, that is a totally different set of issues that needs a different response. That said, aid has had some positive effects here as well but also some very disruptive ones. We can think of aid like a high-pressure fire hose; if you have a fire that is exactly what you want, but if you are trying to get a drink or water your garden it may have some positive effects but it will also knock you down and destroy your plants and most of the water will be wasted. You would need a different approach.

However, this chapter is not about aid but about government, it is just that development aid and government are so closely tied that I needed to discuss it, the number of Christians who look for government or private aid as the primary way to address and solve poverty issues may lead many to conclude that the Bible mandates an active and significant role for government and this conclusion would be fundamentally incorrect.

## A BRIEF REVIEW OF PRE-DEUTERONOMY GOVERNMENT IN THE BIBLE

In the earliest stages of human society government looked different, it was an extension of the family structure expanding into tribal arrangements and eventually small city-states which, in some cases, united, voluntarily or by force, to form kingdoms. These were very fluid due to conquests, trade patterns, and shifting alliances. In the midst of these various economic and political arrangements there were and still are nomads who were primarily shepherds and self-organized usually around a familial structure. We see all of this in the pre-Deuteronomy Bible.

Of course, the main story we follow is of Abraham and his descendants who were nomadic shepherds but through his story we see him battle with a confederation of city-states in Canaan (led by Sodom), visit the kingdom of Egypt already united and led by a pharaoh, interact with the king of the stand-alone city-state of Salem, and, as discussed in a previous chapter, negotiate a land deal. We also see signs of urbanization and the fluidity of these relationships as Abraham's nephew Lot goes from being a nomad shepherd to a city leader in Sodom and Abraham's grandson goes from being a nomadic shepherd to a settled farmer in Egypt.

It was not until the Exodus that the nation of Israel needed its own independent political leadership, which came in the form of a prophet named Moses. Moses had a unique role, he was not a king or a general or even a priest. He had no position that traditionally resulted in political power in that time, he had been raised in the palace but was a stuttering shepherd on the run for crimes he had committed and furthermore was married to a non-Jew. Other than his possible education there was nothing about Moses that said "leadership of Israel." We would see this model repeated with David centuries later.

Moses had many roles and tasks over his forty years of leading Israel, many of them spiritual in nature ranging from writing the Torah to serving as the man between the people and God. But his political role was rather limited. First, he delivered the law at Mount Sinai just a few months after Israel left Egypt. The law had been delivered to him from God so Moses' role was primarily stenography and delivery. Second, he was a judge. This role was a heavy burden for part of it involved instructing the people in the law and then deciding their disputes. It is here that we see the first hints of a more extensive government structure and comes in the form of advice from a non-Israelite:

> The next day Moses sat to judge the people, and the people stood around Moses from morning till evening. When Moses' father-in-law saw all that he was doing for the people, he said, "What is this that you are doing for the people? Why do you sit alone, and all the people stand around you from morning till evening?" And Moses said to his father-in-law, "Because the people come to me to inquire of God; when they have a dispute, they come to me and I decide between one person and another, and I make them know the statutes of God and his laws." Moses' father-in-law said to him, "What you are doing is not good. You and the people with you will certainly wear yourselves out, for the thing is too heavy for you. You are not able to do it alone. Now obey my voice; I will give you advice, and God be with you! You shall represent the people before God and bring their cases to God, and you shall warn them about the statutes and the laws, and make them know the way in which they must walk and what they must do. Moreover, look for able men from all the people, men who fear God, who are trustworthy and hate a bribe, and place such men over the people as chiefs of thousands,

> of hundreds, of fifties, and of tens. And let them judge the people at all times. Every great matter they shall bring to you, but any small matter they shall decide themselves. So it will be easier for you, and they will bear the burden with you. If you do this, God will direct you, you will be able to endure, and all this people also will go to their place in peace." So Moses listened to the voice of his father-in-law and did all that he had said. Moses chose able men out of all Israel and made them heads over the people, chiefs of thousands, of hundreds, of fifties, and of tens. And they judged the people at all times. Any hard case they brought to Moses, but any small matter they decided themselves. Then Moses let his father-in-law depart, and he went away to his own country.[1]

In this we see the first development of a structure that could be called a civil government, or more specifically a judicial system. This is all Israel had, even in Deuteronomy where much more detail and explanation is given this judicial function is the only civil government institution in Israel until they requested a king in 1 Samuel over four hundred years later.

## DEUTERONOMY AND GOVERNMENT: NOT A THEOCRACY

I need to clarify a common misconception; Israel was not a theocracy, which I am sure will surprise some. But Deuteronomy does not set up a true theocracy, at least not as the modern term is used. A *theocracy* is defined as "a form of government in which God or a deity is recognized as the supreme civil ruler, the God's or deity's laws being interpreted by the ecclesiastical authorities."[2] In this sense Israel was a theocracy, God was seen as the supreme ruler. But the more modern usage applies the second definition, "a system of government by priests claiming a divine commission."[3] In this sense Israel was not a theocracy, nor was it any sort of kingdom at least at first. It was a more nuanced political arrangement than is commonly assumed that could be described as a radical departure from the prevailing political-economic arrangements of the era. In a theocracy the priestly class also holds political power. This was the situation in Egypt where the Pharaohs were considered a god and the high priest and in Rome after Augustus when the Caesars were deified. In Israel God establishes a clear separation between the priestly class and the political leadership, Moses was the only one that combined the two roles.

The priests were to come exclusively from the tribe of Levi as detailed in Deuteronomy 21: "Then the priests, the sons of Levi, shall come forward, for the LORD your God has chosen them to minister to him and to bless in the name of the LORD, and by their word every dispute and every assault shall be settled."[4] The Levite priests were to minister and serve as judges but they were not to be political leaders. The political leadership was to come from the tribe of Judah as explained in Genesis 49: "Judah, your brothers shall praise you; your hand shall be on the neck of your enemies; father's sons shall bow down before you. . . . The scepter shall not depart from Judah, the ruler's staff from between his feet, until tribute comes to him; and to him shall be the obedience of the peoples."[5] This is a somewhat ancient and poetic way to describe the fact that the tribe of Judah will produce the kings, in reference to the scepter and staff, symbols used to this day by some European monarchs to demonstrate the power of the state.

But there were further restrictions on the priests; the priests were forbidden to own land. They were allotted forty-eight cities scattered throughout the nation but with no geographically unified and identifiable territory as described in Joshua 21. They were largely dependent on the giving of the other members of the nation for their food and income as described in Numbers 18. The priests had no power to tax or force the people to pay them the only way they got these incomes and offering to use is if they served well and the people stayed faithful. If they served poorly and the people stopped giving, they would suffer. The priests had power and influence in one part of the nation's life and were completely powerless in every other aspect. God places a significant boundary on these powerful people that was meant to restrict them which seems to imply that too much power even in the hands of a faithful priest, is a dangerous thing.

Most of what God has to say about civil government as an institution is contained as warnings. While Deuteronomy does not establish a theocracy, it does not really establish any civil government beyond the aforementioned judges. There is no executive of any form, no police, no legislature, no standing army or any other governmental institution. This would, hundreds of years later, lead to discontent and unrest as the people would eventually demand a governmental structure in the form of a monarchy, so they could be like all the other nations. I will explore that episode later but it is interesting that God calls this a rejection of him. But, anticipating that day, God gives this warning to Israel and by extension to all nations about their leadership and what they should expect and demand from them:

> When you come to the land that the Lord your God is giving you, and you possess it and dwell in it and then say, 'I will set a king over me, like all the nations that are around me,' you may indeed set a king over you whom the Lord your God will choose. One from among your brothers you shall set as king over you. You may not put a foreigner over you, who is not your brother. Only he must not acquire many horses for himself or cause the people to return to Egypt in order to acquire many horses, since the Lord has said to you, 'You shall never return that way again.' And he shall not acquire many wives for himself, lest his

> heart turn away, nor shall he acquire for himself excessive silver and gold. And when he sits on the throne of his kingdom, he shall write for himself in a book a copy of this law, approved by the Levitical priests. And it shall be with him, and he shall read in it all the days of his life, that he may learn to fear the Lord his God by keeping all the words of this law and these statutes, and doing them, that his heart may not be lifted up above his brothers, and that he may not turn aside from the commandment, either to the right hand or to the left, so that he may continue long in his kingdom, he and his children, in Israel.[6]

This passage contains several principles for political leadership and they all point to a government with significant limits, which I explore next.

## A FELLOW COUNTRYMAN

The first principle is that a leader should come from one's own people. A native leader does not guarantee competent and efficient leadership but being ruled by a foreign power comes with problems. There needs to be a sovereign link between the governor and the governed. This link can be broken in many ways and the most obvious and complete break is to actually have a foreign king. While the text does not address the issue, it seems that converts would be acceptable as was the case of Caleb as explained in a previous chapter. But another aspect of this, that many nations experienced throughout history, is to have a fellow countryman in leadership but who has sworn an oath to another, a vassal state or a puppet that just implements and enforces what others have decided. In times past this may be a king who swore allegiance to another to avoid a war or was set up as a puppet ruler after a military defeat. In more recent times this could be leaders who were supported by other countries with money and arms as long as the ruler stayed friendly and compliant with the supplier of that money and arms. Large superpower nations used this method frequently to rent loyalty during the Cold War and still do to some extent.

For many of the developing nations this principle is being violated by the relationship between the government and the World Bank and International Monetary Fund. As Ghanaian entrepreneur Herman Chinery-Hesse (see Appendix A for a biography) stated in the excellent video series called *Poverty Cure*, the government of many developing nations is often more interested in a smile on the World Bank country director's face than it is with the success of his (Chinery-Hesse's) business.[7] Dambisa Moyo (see Appendix A for a biography), the excellent Zimbabwean economist, makes the same point in her book *Dead Aid*. In it she makes the somewhat surprising claim that while some aid has done good things it is still destructive in the long term because it makes people of the developing nation look to the government of the aid donor and completely jettison the notion that their own government may have a duty and actually be capable of providing public goods and services.[8] This thesis upset Bill Gates quite a bit and he said that Moyo was not very educated about aid and that she was immoral, promoting evil and her ideas are actually killing people.[9] Strong aid advocates see only the positive things aid has done and cannot see the damage and harm, which may be hard to see. It is hard to see shoe businesses that are not started because TOMS floods the market with free shoes from time to time. Helping some very identifiable people, like medical help for the sick, is easy to see; severing the links between people and their institutions and the long-term effects are diffused and very hard to see. It takes a deeper understanding of the issue than Gates seems to exhibit. While Gates's position, to give aid to the needy, sounds moral, after all he says so himself, Moyo's point is actually much more consistent with the biblical principle. Human allegiance naturally extends to the one providing the things we need: children to parents, employees to employer, citizen to government. These are very different relationships and there is much more to each of them but one aspect is that there are needs to be met and one party is responsible for meeting the needs of the other. If a parent, employer, or government fails or seems unable to meet its responsibility, the child, employee, and citizen will naturally look elsewhere and their allegiances will soon follow.

## A SMALL ARMY AND NO ENTANGLING ALLIANCES

The second principle we see is that the king should not have many horses. In this day and age that is not literally an issue but there is of course more to this than making sure a nation is not ruled by a person with an equine problem. Owning a large number of horses implied several things: wealth, ownership of large amounts of property to keep them, people to care for them, but the most important implication is that horses were the most advanced war weapon of the day. This restriction on the king's horses was a way to keep the standing army small. Throughout history a government with a large standing army has done two things: invade other countries and/or oppress his own people. God wanted no such behavior. There is a faith element in this, Israel was to trust God as its protector, but there is also a practical aspect; a king cannot be tempted to misuse what he does not have. We see this misuse implied in a famous later episode with Israel's most famous king, David. In the chain of events that results in David taking another man's wife, Bathsheba, having her husband killed, and then being confronted by the prophet Nathan, what is often overlooked is how it all began; "In the spring of the year, the time when kings go out to battle, David sent Joab, and his servants with him, and all Israel. And they ravaged the Ammonites and besieged Rabbah. But David remained at Jerusalem."[10] There was an understood time when kings would go and fight each other, David was not with his army like a good king would be when it was in the field. If he had kept his army home in an effort to forge peace that would have been something else but it was just David who stayed home apparently to check out his soldiers' wives. But the bigger issue is that he had an army at all, and Israel wanted to be like the other nations, so when spring came off to war they went. Besides the temptation to use one's army, it is also very expensive to maintain a standing army. Having a large group of largely young men in dedicated service to training for and engaging in combat takes those very productive men away from producing other goods and services and of course requires that they be fed, clothed, and equipped. The direct costs of keeping them fed, equipped, and paid were high and the opportunity costs of all that lost production may have been higher.

But there are bad people in the world and some of the run countries and have armies and if we have no army we are asking for problems from our neighbors, right? This is true and Israel experienced that as well with the Philistines and some other nations. There is a difference between being prepared to address bad people and having a standing army. During Solomon's reign we have no record of any significant military conflict, Solomon was a trader and explorer, much more the merchant king then the mercenary king his father, David, was. Solomon was not without his problems but he did manage to operate in a hostile neighborhood effectively by engaging in trade with his neighbors. In modern times we can look to a nation like Switzerland for a similar approach. A country that maintains strict neutrality but whose people are trained and prepared in military skills as a civilian-based armed force, but whose standing professional army is very small. So, Switzerland trades with all, invades none, defends well, and is very wealthy. Not a bad model.

This verse also puts a restriction on the number of wives the king may acquire. Like with horses this is deeper than avoiding a polygamous leader, although that is true as well. But in those days as well as up to recent times, royal weddings were often diplomatic acts and treaty making. A foreign king will be less likely to invade the home country of his wife or son-in-law. This is where Solomon got in trouble with his nearly 1,000 wives and concubines. But this prohibition can remind one of Thomas Jefferson's admonition to have friendship with all nations and entangling alliances with none, a philosophy loosely akin to warnings about foreign alliances in George Washington's farewell address. A significant part of the concern for Israel was that foreign nations did not worship the true God and therefore did not have the same value system, culture, and beliefs and there was real spiritual danger in that. But, as always, there is a practical side which is that a permanent alliance can draw a nation into a mess of one sort or another that they had nothing to do with and want nothing to do with. One may end up defending an immoral position, a losing position, or even end up the taking the brunt of the fallout as can be argued happened to Germany in World War I, a war started between Serbia and Germany's ally Austria-Hungary ended up ruining Germany for the next seventy years.

## LIMITED WEALTH

The next prohibition on the king was a restriction that he should not acquire much silver and gold. This prohibition has several implications. One is that the king should not be engaging in excessive taxation, taking from the people their rightful earnings and wealth and transferring it to the king (state) for non-productive uses such as extra palaces, building projects, and so forth. Centuries later, when Israel demands a king and is on the verge of appointing one, the prophet Samuel expounds upon this warning in great detail:

> So Samuel told all the words of the Lord to the people who were asking for a king from him. He said, "These will be the ways of the king who will reign over you: he will take your sons and appoint them to his chariots and to be his horsemen and to run before his chariots. And he will appoint for himself commanders of thousands and commanders of fifties, and some to plow his ground and to reap his harvest, and to make his implements of war and the equipment of his chariots. He will take your daughters to be perfumers and cooks and bakers. He will take the best of your fields and vineyards and olive orchards and give them to his servants. He will take the tenth of your grain and of your vineyards and give it to his officers and to his servants. He will take your male servants and female servants and the best of your young men and your donkeys, and put them to his work. He will take the tenth of your flocks, and you shall be his slaves. And in that day you will cry out because of your king, whom you have chosen for yourselves, but the Lord will not answer you in that day."
>
> But the people refused to obey the voice of Samuel. And they said, "No! But there shall be a king over us, that we also may be like all the nations, and that our king may judge us and go out before us and fight our battles."[11]

Samuel warns Israel of the high cost of having a king in great detail which includes conscription and forced service, taxation of land and other property, and outright slavery. But Israel in some sort combination of patriotic fervor, spiritual unfaithfulness, and fear demanded a king.

While Deuteronomy 17 and the passage in 1 Samuel imply low taxes and warn against high taxes, the Bible does not actually say much about taxation itself. We have some hints but no definitive statement on tax structure or rates. Romans 13 does state that the faithful should pay their taxes and Jesus uses a miracle to pay the temple tax in Matthew 17. While suggestive, it is by no means definitive, that the few times the Bible seems to deal with taxation issues it is a proportional or flat tax ranging from 10 percent as in the case of Abraham with Melchizedek, the king of Salem, in Genesis 14 or the tithe in Deuteronomy 14 and other passages, to 20 percent as in the case of Joseph in Egypt in Genesis 41.

Another implication of this warning is the king will be corrupt. Power attracts certain kinds of people and tends to be corrupting, fallen man, no matter how well intentioned is very susceptible to abusing power. We see this throughout the Bible and throughout history. It is the lesson of *The Lord of the Rings* and many other literary works. We see corruption in politics and government throughout the world, however, it is often most vividly on display in the developing world and frequently in systems that claim to value people such as socialism.[12] Professor George Ayittey calls them Swiss Bank Socialists,[13] who claim they are implementing socialism for the people but are actually accumulating large amounts of wealth for themselves and storing it out of the country. Below is Table 2.6.1 of the wealthiest leaders in Africa and the nation's per capital GDP, it tells a sad and depressing story.

**Table 2.6.1. Wealthiest African Political Leaders**

| *Nation* | *Leader* | *Net Worth*[a] | *Years in Power* | *National GDP*[b] | *Per Capita GDP*[b] |
|---|---|---|---|---|---|
| Angola | Jose Eduardo dos Santos | $20 billion | 1979–2017 | $192 billion | $6,800 |
| Morocco | Mohammed VI | $5.8 billion | 1999–present | $300.1 billion | $8,600 |
| Equatorial Guinea | Teodoro Obiang Nguema Mbasogo | $600 million | 1979–present | $29.38 billion | $34,900[e] |
| Kenya | Uhuru Kenyatta[c] | $500 million | 2013–present | $163.4 billion | $3,500 |
| Cameroon | Paul Biya | $200 million | 1982–present | $81.5 billion | $3,400 |
| Kingdom of Eswantini[d] | Mswati III | $200 million | 1986–present | $11.3 billion | $9,900 |
| Chad | Idriss Déby | $50 million | 1990–present | $9.6 billion | $2,400 |

a. Estimates from *Forbes* Magazine
b. GDP figures from CIA World Fact Book (national figures for purchasing power parity)[1]
c. Kenyatta is a political legacy, son of the founder of the independent state of Kenya
d. Formerly known as Swaziland
e. Equatorial Guinea has 44% of the population below the poverty line, the GDP number is highly skewed

1. Central Intelligence Agency, *The World Factbook*, n.d., https://www.cia.gov/library/publications/the-world-factbook/geos/sn.html.

There are other wealthy leaders of course, the Sultan of Brunei is supposedly the world's richest leader with a net worth of $30 billion but his nation's per capita GDP is over $70,000. American presidents are frequently rich, both Donald Trump and Barack Obama were or are among the richest world leaders. The point is not that the leader is rich but how the leader gets rich. In a previous chapter I criticized former president Harry Truman but he supposedly made the statement that anyone who gets rich in politics is a crook and that is the point. If the leader became wealthy as a result of being leader, as all the leaders in the Table 2.6.1 did, then they are abusing their power and position. But we should not think it is only the top office that engages in such behavior, the legislators like to get in on the money as well. A list of the highest-paid national legislatures (Parliaments, Congresses, etc.) shows some expected countries like the United States, Switzerland, and New Zealand but also some surprises. Table 2.6.2 below gives some comparisons of legislative compensation.

As is obvious from Table 2.6.2, some developing nations pay their legislators well. There is much discussion these days about income inequality and how business leaders should cap their salaries at a certain rate above the average worker's pay. I am not debating that point but the Bible is clear that

**Table 2.6.2. Compensation for Selected National Legislatures**

| *Country* | *Annual Salary* | *Per Capita GDP*[1] | *Ratio of salary to GDP* |
|---|---|---|---|
| Singapore[a] | >$1,000,000 | $90,500 | 11 |
| South Africa | $194,916[2] | $13,400 | 14.5 |
| Nigeria | $189,600[3] | $5,900 | 32 |
| Italy[b] | $182,000[4] | $38,000 | 4.8 |
| United States | $165,200[c] | $59,500 | 2.7 |
| Kenya | $164,880[5] | $3,500 | 47 |
| Switzerland | $141,500[d] | $61,400 | 2.3 |
| Uganda | $104,500 | $2,400 | 43.5 |

a. Singapore has the highest paid government officials in the world but the salary is hard to pinpoint since some of it is tied to economic performance of the city-state.
b. Italy is the highest paid of the European legislatures.
c. Leadership earns more with the top salary for the Speaker of the House at $212,000.
d. Members of the Swiss Federal Assembly earn between 130,000 and 150,000 CHF a year depending on how many days the Assembly meets. The figure in the table was based on the exchange rates on July 6, 2018 for 140,000 CHF.

1. Central Intelligence Agency, *The World Factbook*, n.d., https://www.cia.gov/library/publications/the-world-factbook/geos/sn.html.
2. Mark Babatunde, "Africa's Highest Paid Members of Parliament," *Face2face Africa*, February 5, 2018.
3. Ibid.
4. Annalisa Merelli, "In Italy, Members of Parliament Make Five Times More than the Average Worker," *Quartz Ideas*, March 4, 2014, https://qz.com/183305/in-italy-members-of-parliament-make-five-times-more-than-the-average-worker/.
5. Babatunde, "Africa's Highest Paid Members of Parliament."

there are dangers when the government officials are so much wealthier than the people they govern and while it does not give a ratio or guideline on what is too much gold or silver, it is safe to say that if one of the best ways to get wealthy is by becoming part of the government then the country in question is probably in trouble.

## UNDER THE LAW

The final qualification we see is that the king or government must know and follow the law. If we accept the proposition that Deuteronomy is a constitution then we get two clear principles for modern government from this command; the government should be under the constitution and the government must know and respect the constitution.

Being under the constitution is a tricky requirement. Only Israel had a constitution handed down from God, everyone else has a man-made constitution, which is subject to errors and issues and needs to be updated and adjusted as time goes by. But the current government of any country should not be able to change the constitution easily or in ways that serve its own narrow purposes. Many in the developing world have had leaders change the election requirements or term limits so they can stay in office indefinitely. The African Center for Strategic Studies has produced this chart[14] to show the problem in Africa.

The Center summarizes the table like this:

- Eighteen African countries have established a constitutional two-term limit on their executive office holders. Chief executives in these countries have been in power for less than four years, on average.
- Ten African leaders have evaded term limit restrictions. The average time in power for leaders in these countries is twenty-one years.
- Eight of the ten countries where term limits have been undone are in Central Africa.
- Southern Africa is the sub-region with the strongest adherence to term limits.
- Term limits for leaders in North and East Africa largely remain weak or absent.[15]

The desire to cling to power and the arrogance to change the laws enable it is a violation of God's command to make sure the leader's heart is not raised above his brothers and such actions have material consequences as the state is the focus of society and uses an ever increasing share of resources. There is good news as some nations are starting to see turnover in political office, but it is no accident that many on the list of rich rulers above are also on the list

AFRICA CENTER FOR STRATEGIC STUDIES

## Constitutional Term Limits for African Leaders

| No Constitutional Two-Term Limit | Countries with Two-Term Limit in Constitution | | | | |
|---|---|---|---|---|---|
| | Limit Not Yet Met by Any President (Year Limit to Be Reached) | Limit Not Retroactively Applied to Current Executive | Two-Term Limit Reached | | |
| | | | Attempted Modification or Elimination of Limit | | Left Office (First Leader to Adhere to Limit) |
| | | | Successful | Unsuccessful | |
| Cape Verde[1] (three-term limit) | Liberia (2017) | Algeria[4] | Togo (Eyadéma, 2002) | Zambia (Chiluba, 2001) | Tanzania (Mwinyi, 1995) |
| Equatorial Guinea | Côte d'Ivoire (2018) | Zimbabwe[5] | Gabon (Bongo, 2003) | Malawi (Muluzi, 2003) | Ghana (Rawlings, 2001) |
| Eritrea | Mauritania (2019) | | Uganda (Museveni, 2005) | Nigeria (Obasanjo, 2006) | São Tomé and Príncipe (Trovoada, 2001) |
| Ethiopia[1] | Guinea (2020) | | Chad (Deby, 2005) | Niger (Tandja, 2009) | Kenya (Moi, 2002) |
| Gambia | Egypt (2022) | | Cameroon (Biya, 2008) | Senegal (Wade, 2012) | Mozambique (Chissano, 2005) |
| Guinea-Bissau | Madagascar (2024) | | Djibouti (Guellah, 2010) | Burkina Faso (Compaoré, 2014) | Benin (Kérékou, 2006) |
| Lesotho[1] | Tunisia (2024) | | Rwanda (Kagame, 2015) | | Comoros (Assoumani, 2006) |
| Mauritius[1] | Central African Republic (2026) | | Burundi (Nkurunziza, 2015)[6] | | Sierra Leone (Kabbah, 2007) |
| Morocco[2] | Angola (2027) | | Republic of Congo (Nguesso, 2015) | | Botswana (Mogae, 2008) |
| Seychelles (three-term limit) | Libya[3] | | DRC (Kabila, 2016)[7] | | Mali (Konaré, 2008) |
| Somalia | | | | | South Africa (Mbeki, 2008) |
| South Sudan | | | | | Namibia (Pohamba, 2015) |
| Sudan | | | | | |
| Swaziland[2] | | | | | |

[1] Executive authority largely rests with the office of the prime minister, which does not face any restrictions on tenure.

[2] Executive authority rests with a monarch.

[3] Libya: The draft 2016 Constitution imposes two-term limits.

[4] Algeria: The term-limit clause was removed in 2008 for Abdelaziz Bouteflika to run again and reinstated in 2016 as he serves out his last term.

[5] Zimbabwe: The Constitution adopted in 2013 introduced a two-term limit. Robert Mugabe is due to run for his second term in 2018.

[6] Burundi: While legitimacy remains contested, Pierre Nkurunziza has held onto power past term limit expiration in 2015.

[7] DRC: Joseph Kabila served out his second term in 2016 but negotiated to stay on until December 2017.

*Updated September 2017*

**Figure 6.1. Constitutional Term Limits for African Leaders**

Africa Center for Strategic Studies

of leaders with no term limits or have managed to evade them somehow. And this is not to isolate Africa as unique, many nations around the world have had leaders hang on to power for long periods of time; some economic success stories include Lee Kuan Yew governing Singapore for thirty years, and some were less successful economic stories such as Sukarno ruling Indonesia for twenty-two years and Ferdinand Marcos ruling the Philippines for thirty-one years. Power is seductive and the desire to hold on to it can be very strong, even in the supposed open and free West, it is not unusual to have legislators serving twenty years or more with many seeing triple digit increases in their personal net worth while in office.

## REFORMS?

There is a small but vocal intellectual movement alive in the United States and elsewhere that has reacted to the abuses of government by calling for an abolition of government. This group is sometimes known as anarcho-capitalists. And, of course there have been a few notable anarchists of all sorts throughout history. Those who have experienced, observed, or studied the massive abuse of large tyrannical governments of the twentieth century can certainly have some sympathy to this view. Even those who see the small everyday abuses of the Congressman engaging in insider trading and the bribes needed to get stuff done, rigged elections and so forth even in prosperous countries can find it debilitating and draining on the economy and the public spirit as expressed as declining confidence in government and civil processes all over the world.

However, as sympathetic as one can be to this position, and a number of Christians[16] have been, it does not seem to me that the Bible is congruent with anarchy of any sort. There is government within the family, the Jewish community, the church, and civil society. Romans 13 is clear that government is instituted, when acting properly, to encourage good and punish evil. It is important to understand what that passage also does not say as well and it should be read in conjunction with 1 Samuel 8 abut the abuses of government. When the government's role, limitations, and potential abuses are considered in their entirety and read with other verses about caring for the elderly and widows as discussed in previous chapters, we get a very different picture of government's role then has developed in the West and seems to be developing in other nations. Nowhere does any verse make the welfare of the downtrodden the responsibility of the government, yet the majority of the budgets in all Western nations is spent on just those tasks, tasks that the Bible explicitly assigned to other institutions, primarily the family but also the church. If one wonders why welfare programs are so wasteful and poorly administered and do not seem to actually achieve the goal of alleviating poverty then maybe it is because the wrong institution has taken over the task. As Abraham Kuyper pointed out there are spheres in society with their created or ordained purpose such as government, family, church, and commerce. When one sphere encroaches on another and tries to do a task it was not created to do, it does that task poorly and often crowds out the rightful and better equipped sphere from performing the task.[17] Plus, when one sphere is trying to do things it is not well suited for that diverts resources from what it should be doing and it goes on a quest to obtain more resources, which could be through taxation for government, consumer credit for families, and so on.

The Bible has a clear and specific role for government. First, to punish evil and promote good as we see in Romans 13. After that, the Bible spends much of the space devoted to the discussion of government in placing restrictions on it and warning us about its abuses. There was no concern about the government underperforming or being too timid in performing its functions, once a person has power, he will use it and the concern is always about abuse. Based on these warnings and restrictions a smaller government with well-defined and limited duties, answerable to the people and operating under the law, would seem to fit the biblical ideal of what leads to flourishing and prosperity for the people.

## NOTES

1. *Exodus*, n.d., 18:13–24 (ESV).
2. *Dictionary.Com*, n.d., http://www.dictionary.com/browse/theocracy.
3. Ibid.
4. *Deuteronomy*, n.d., 21:5 (ESV).
5. *Genesis*, n.d., 49:8–10 (ESV).
6. *Deuteronomy*, 17:14–20 (ESV).
7. Michael Miller, *Poverty Cure*, vol. 1, 6 vols. (Grand Rapids, MI: Acton Media, 2012), http://povertycure.org/.
8. Dambisa Moyo, Is Aid Killing Africa? Dambisa Moyo talks Dead Aid on ABC, March 17, 2009, https://www.youtube.com/watch?v=HIPvlQOCfAQ&t=192s.
9. Bill Gates, Interview with Bill Gates, May 29, 2013, https://www.youtube.com/watch?v=5utDdxveaJc.
10. *2 Samuel*, n.d., 11:1 (ESV).
11. *1 Samuel*, n.d., 8:10–21 (ESV.
12. *Socialism* is a term for a wide collection of political-economic systems in which the means of production are owned by some sort of collective body such as the tribe, community, or country, with practical decision-making in the hands of the

government apparatus. Currently, a popular form in the West is Democratic-Socialism which proposes collective ownership of the means of production and economic decisions subject to a vote of the people or their representatives. Proponents of this system frequently claim it is morally superior to other systems since it purports to be more inclusive and eliminates major sources of inequality such as private property and private profits.

13. *George Ayittey: Cheetahs v. Hippos for Africa's Future*, TED Talk (Tanzania, 2007), https://www.youtube.com/watch?v=ZnepHUYFqgg&t=41s.

14. African Center for Strategic Studies, "Constitutional Term Limits for African Leaders" (Washington, D.C., September 14, 2017), https://africacenter.org/spotlight/constitutional-term-limits-african-leaders/.

15. Ibid.

16. I am not looking to mischaracterize anyone's statements or beliefs but J.R.R. Tolkien and Leo Tolstoy are two notable figures who expressed both strong Christian beliefs and at least sympathy for some aspects of anarchist thinking.

17. Many of Kuyper's writings are still in Dutch only but are being translated but there are some English treatments including Jordan Ballor's book *Why Kuyper Matters.*

## *Chapter Seven*

# Trade and Markets

For this discussion I will reference quite a few passages outside of Deuteronomy as much of the direct evidence for the notion that the Bible prefers a market arrangement over a collective or centralized one is located outside of the book of Deuteronomy. It is formed in Israel's experience not in its explicit rules. However, there is significant circumstantial evidence to support the idea that the Bible is a market-friendly text in Deuteronomy and even outside of the biblical account.

Before I present the biblical support for markets and trade, I want to begin by dispelling a long-standing philosophy within Christian and Jewish circles dating back to nearly the beginning of the biblical narrative and continuing up to this very day and that is the desire to be self-sufficient. The spiritual desire to live a more holy life and be different from unbelievers has regularly led to a practical application of actually physically separating oneself from the larger society. It has led to the communities such as the one at Qumran of Dead Sea Scrolls fame, established by the Essenes in the second century B.C. and some of the monastic traditions (though certainly not all) throughout Europe down to this very day where there is a sub-culture of Christians that advocate 'living off the grid' in what some call personal secession either individually or in small communities of like-minded people. I am not questioning their motivations and what pushed them to make this decision, but we know that God designed people to live in community and not be physically separated from others. The people in these sorts of off-the-grid communities would probably argue that they are not isolating themselves from others, they are forming and living in communities with others. And that is true, they are not some caricature hermit taking a vow of silence and poverty living in the desert, but they are separating themselves in significant and deliberate ways.

Some of the first words we attribute to God is about it not being good for man to be alone which leads to the formation of the family to tribes, to nations and then communities within the nation such as cities and of course temples and later churches. These are all communities that God approves of in the Bible and in many cases ordains and creates himself. In addition to this, six of the Ten Commandments are about how we are to interact with each other, responsibilities and restraints on our behavior toward our neighbors (which is everyone), and large parts of Deuteronomy and what we have discussed in this book expound upon those commandments and explain their application. In short, we are not like tigers who live primarily solitary lives but more like ants, as Proverbs 6, written by Solomon whom I will spend more time on below, tells us to be like:

> Go to the ant, O sluggard; consider her ways, and be wise.
> Without having any chief, officer, or ruler, she prepares her bread in summer and gathers her food in harvest.[1, 2]

Besides learning how to be industrious this passage is also a perfect picture of an emergent market order, a social system in which every member is free to follow his or her own interests and skills to serve the other members of society and try to earn a profit doing so and as an unintended result society is better off. The ant colony survives because each ant wants to survive the winter and prepares to do so, the city survives because each person want to flourish and takes actions to do so that unintentionally benefit others. There is more to this verse than an admonition against laziness, this is the way to live in community.

So, you may be saying of course we are not to be lazy, but how does this passage support the idea of a market order? We can be diligent and industrious in any kind of system, right? Obviously, the answer to this is yes, just as one can be lazy in any system but the question is which system rewards work best, allows one to have the most meat in summer and gather the most food in harvest, or to phrase it another way, which system promotes, encourages, and rewards good stewardship? What is God's preferred economic arrangement? To a large extent we have answered this in a previous chapter, God is very interested in private property and protecting property rights, that eliminates collectivist schemes such as socialism, communism, and command schemes such as fascism and certain kinds of monarchy arrangements.

But it is possible to have a system of private property and not have a market system. It is possible for each family to have a plot of land that is legally well protected but endeavor to be self-sufficient without much commerce with anyone else. This could be the arrangement God had in mind for Israel, a plethora of self-sufficient farmers, we have an abundance of evidence that suggests otherwise, but what might that system look like today? This may well be the model modern Christian off-the-grid types have in mind, as this advertisement from off-grid.net suggests:

> I am a home owner in San Mateo Ca and wanting to plan to sell and buy an off grid home in north eastern CA or somewhere away from the coast and away from the cities within a few hours' drive of the bay area CA. I would like to be near other Christians who are also off grid and not too far from a small town and medical services for my elderly parents when needs arise. Also important to have a good place to grow lots of food and my own water source. Please contact me if you have any thoughts to help.[3]

While God may want people to spend time alone in the wilderness, it is in preparation for serving better. Those in the wilderness go there to learn, commune with God, be alone without distractions, but then always return to the community. Isolation is not to be a permanent lifestyle. Moses, David, Elijah, Jesus, Paul, and others all had wilderness experiences that usually came right before they went to their respective communities to serve, minister, teach, and lead. They never stayed there.

But before I get ahead of myself, I need to define what a market system is and what is required for it to function properly. Then I can show where we see these things in the Bible. A market system is a social organization that is elegantly simple to use with aspects of it manifested in the natural world; in reality it is a complex, intricate network of cooperating and competing entities that frequently span the globe to deliver the simplest product but at its core it is two people engaging in exchange or trade and no one has to be taught how to engage in trade. We can observe trading among very young children, even before they can talk and even in some animals and certainly among all peoples throughout history where they have not been prevented from doing so. A market system naturally emerges which is why it does not need to be designed and explains the lack of actual system design specifics in Deuteronomy. Other than the freedom to act, to engage others voluntarily, the only other requirements for a market to emerge is private property. People naturally have differing production abilities and differing consumption desires or what economists call tastes and preferences which drives the desire to seek out trades. To put it as simple as possible, people like more things than they can produce, so if we have the freedom to trade and stuff to trade, the rest will take care of itself.

## THE MODERN SELF-SUFFICIENCY MYTH

I would like to start the discussion about how vital trade is in the same way I start my lectures on the subject; imagine you are all alone surrounded by all the best natural resources you could imagine. Except we can do a little better here with the supposed self-sufficient off-the-grid types we already met earlier. They are able to live that way with minimal degradation to their lifestyle because the United States is wealthy, markets are well developed, and the cost to enter that lifestyle is relatively low as is the cost to reverse that decision should they so choose. In other words, it is something of a luxury available due to the fact that most people do *not* live in that lifestyle and they can choose just how much off-the-grid they care to be. The fact that they have internet groups and organize via the web shows they are not that far off and to be fair many of them talk about not so much being off-the-grid but on a separate grid that they control. In the United States a better example of off-the-grid may be the Amish. There are various versions of Amish but as a general rule they avoid many modern conveniences, do not use electricity, have their own schools, learn their own version of German as a first language, and do not participate in the broader community (the English as they call the non-Amish) very much although they do still engage in commerce with the English. The Amish are characterized as hardworking and industrious but even they are better off by being in a modern economy. If one drives through Lancaster or York Counties in Pennsylvania, where there is a large concentration of Amish, one will see horse hitching posts at the local, and I might add fully electrified, grocery and hardware stores. Neither of these are what I mean by self-sufficiency, these are carved-out communities that still have significant, if fewer, ties to the larger community.

## REAL SELF-SUFFICIENCY MEANS POVERTY

True self-sufficiency is characterized by a lack of trade. People are producing all they consume and consume nothing else. The lone survivor of a shipwreck (Robinson Crusoe) or plane crash (Chuck Noland from *Castaway*), these guys are poor, desperate, and in one case just a little unstable. While finding these idealized conditions in the real world are rare and exist due to unique circumstances, some countries come closer to this than we might expect and they too are poor. Table 2.7.1 below looks at the ten nations with the highest percent of their population in extreme poverty and five wealthy nations (one from each multi-nation continent) and compares their trading activity with a measure called the Trade Index. The Trade Index is the total U.S. dollar value of a nation's imports and exports added together and divided by the total population. It is not a very sophisticated measure but it gives a sense of how much trading a nation is engaging in and presents it in a per capita way to adjust for population differences. The poor nations have an average Trade Index of $699 and an average of 62.6 percent of their population in extreme poverty. The wealthy nations have an average Trade Index of $49,516 (even without the very strong outlier of Hong Kong the index is still $25,213 which is 36 times that of the poor country average) and an average poverty rate of 15 percent. Wealth and trading go together, not just internal trading but external trading as this table implies.

The extent of a nation's ability to trade is determined by a number of factors, but most are political and legal, people naturally trade. Population may influence it some but Hong Kong is a small political entity and is the most active trader nation in the world on a per capita basis. And many other small population nations are wealthy and active traders as Table 2.7.2 shows:

**Table 2.7.1. Trade and Poverty: Some Comparison of Poor and Wealthy Countries[1]**

| *Country*[a] | *Population* | *Trade Index* | *Percent in Poverty* |
|---|---|---|---|
| Madagascar | 25,054,161 | $257 | 70.7% |
| Zimbabwe | 13,805,804 | $679 | 72.3% |
| Democratic Republic of the Congo | 83,301,151 | $209 | 63.0% |
| Guinea-Bissau | 1,792,338 | $291 | 67.0% |
| Eritrea | 5,918,919 | $298 | 50.0% |
| Burundi | 11,466,756 | $47 | 64.6% |
| Liberia | 4,689,021 | $309 | 54.1% |
| Eswantini | 1,467,152 | $2,112 | 63.0% |
| São Tomé and Príncipe | 201,025 | $689 | 61.7% |
| Honduras | 9,038,741 | $2,103 | 60.0% |
| Hong Kong | 7,191,503 | $146,729 | 19.9% |
| United States | 326,625,791 | $12,026 | 15.1% |
| Chile | 17,789,267 | $6,995 | 14.4% |
| Switzerland | 8,236,303 | $75,701 | 6.60% |
| Botswana | 2,214,858 | $6,130 | 19.30% |

a. Note: Equatorial Guinea and Central African Republic are omitted. Equatorial Guinea's data is highly skewed due to oil revenue that is flowing mostly to the very corrupt government (see the president's net worth above) and CAR does report much data.

1. Central Intelligence Agency, *The World Factbook*, n.d., https://www.cia.gov/library/publications/the-world-factbook/geos/sn.html.

**Table 2.7.2. Small (Wealthy) Nations with Large Trade Indexes[1]**

| *Country* | *GDP per Capita* | *Trade Index* | *Population* |
|---|---|---|---|
| The Bahamas | $25,100 | $12,242 | 329,988 |
| Denmark | $49,600 | $37,070 | 5,605,948 |
| Luxembourg | $109,100 | $68,672 | 594,130 |
| Ireland | $72,600 | $23,655 | 5,011,102 |
| Liechtenstein | $139,100 | $142,245 | 38,244 |

1. Central Intelligence Agency, *The World Factbook*, n.d., https://www.cia.gov/library/publications/the-world-factbook/geos/sn.html.

If we accept that Deuteronomy was a set of rules and principles to enable flourishing, which includes material prosperity, as we discussed in the opening chapter, then the evidence would say that trade is part of God's economic order and if we examine the Bible looking for evidence in support of that hypothesis it is actually quite evident even in the first few chapters of Genesis.

## TRADE BEFORE DEUTERONOMY

Trade is, in part, based on differences in production abilities, differences in opportunity costs, that is how much do we give up of one thing to produce another? These differences in productive capacity lead to comparative advantages, the advantage we have in production compared to others. People and nations trade because it is cheaper to buy something than to make it ourselves, that is we give up fewer opportunities when we buy it rather than to make it. Think about your own personal decision to buy a shirt. Some of you may sew and enjoy it and a few may make all of your own clothes but for most people, making one's own shirt from scratch would be a very time-consuming and expensive task requiring hours of time to learn and do and then the end product would probably not be so good. You would improve over time but how long would that take? If you are better suited for other tasks you practice the highest level of stewardship by doing those tasks you do best and not waste so much time making shirts but buying them. To follow one man's journey in exploring this concept with trying to make his own toaster, I recommend Thomas Thwaites's book (or TED Talk) *The Toaster Project*, in which he tries to make a toaster from scratch, spending nine months and over $1,500 to make an appliance anyone can buy at a store for under $10. This was an education but high opportunity cost project.

So, a sign that there are markets, even if no one is saying "hey, there's a market here!" is when we see specialization, people focused on a narrow range of production, who are producing things they can do well, producing much more than they personally need so they can sell them to others and purchase things they do need but are not producing themselves. Like you and your shirt or toaster. The Bible speaks of specialization almost from word one. In Genesis 4, there is the story of Cain and Abel, a tragic and famous story of brotherly betrayal, and from which we get the awful catchphrase "am I my brother's keeper" (verse 9) as Cain gives God a sarcastic and evil response. However, for economic purposes and what is often ignored is that Cain and Abel already showed that there was specialization and markets in place; "Now Abel was a keeper of sheep, and Cain a worker of the ground. In the course of time Cain brought to the LORD an offering of the fruit of the ground, and Abel also brought of the firstborn of his flock and of their fat portions."[4] We have no idea how well developed the markets were in these earliest days of mankind but we clearly have specialization which implies some level of trading. But a few verses later this concept is presented to us in more detail: "Adah bore Jabal; he was the father of those who dwell in tents and have livestock. His brother's name was Jubal; he was the father of all those who play the lyre and pipe. Zillah also bore Tubal-cain; he was the forger of all instruments of bronze and iron."[5] These tribes were specializing in production and furthermore the existence of arts implies there was enough excess production in food and other essentials that some people were able to turn their attention to culture. This assertion is supported by the fact that this same chapter and chapter 5 discuss about how cities were being established. These were not cities as we think of them, they held probably no more than a few thousand, more likely a few hundred people, but cities, even of this size, can only exist if there is surplus agricultural production which allows some people to engage in other activities such as being a shopkeeper in the city where food must be purchased since it cannot be as easily grown in the more densely populated area.

This is not to imply that the ancient Middle East was an advanced market economy, but it is to imply and I think by the end of this chapter pretty well prove that markets were prevalent, well-used, and that trade was the norm not self-sufficiency. Even Abraham (Abram before Genesis 17) who was a nomad and settled nowhere permanently engaged in trade and we glimpse that as backdrop to other stories. We would expect a nomad to be more self-sufficient but Abraham was more like a small traveling city having hundreds, if not a thousand people under his authority. But we see him buying and selling on several occasions. He also traveled to Egypt and this may not seem like much but keep in mind he was using roads or at least well-established routes used by trading caravans long before Rome built its road system. A few years later Abraham's great-grandsons, in a spiteful act of jealousy, sold one of their own, Joseph, into slavery. While the story is well known and was even the inspiration for a Broadway play, the incident gives us some insight into the economic structure of the day: "And looking up they saw a caravan of Ishmaelites coming from Gilead, with their camels bearing gum, balm, and myrrh, on their way to carry it down to Egypt. Then Judah said to his brothers, 'What profit is it if we kill our brother and conceal his blood? Come, let us sell him to the Ishmaelites, and let not our hand be upon him, for he is our brother, our own flesh.' And his brothers listened to him. Then Midianite traders passed by. And they drew Joseph up and lifted him out of the pit, and sold him to the Ishmaelites for twenty shekels of silver. They took Joseph to Egypt."[6] These traders obviously dealt in many goods they were carrying products from the upper middle east to Egypt and the trade must have been very active indeed as the only places we tend to find myrrh and balm these days are in northern Africa and Saudi Arabia.

It is obvious that even in the earliest days of civilization trade was active and God's people were engaged in it. After Joseph rises to power in Egypt and the famine comes, he *sells* food, as part of a plan God reveals to him. However, these episodes are not the only evidence we have for God's view of trade, as the real estate professionals will tell you, when it comes to land it is all about location.

## THE LOCATION OF THE PROMISED LAND: THE GEOGRAPHY OF THE ANCIENT MIDDLE EAST

In Genesis 15 God promises Abram land for his descendants, what appropriately enough came to be called the Promised Land. It was not a generic promise of some land but a specific promise of a particular tract of land between the Nile and the Euphrates (which by the way is the basis for the modern-day Israeli flag, two blue lines representing the two rivers with the Star of David in between, its design comes from these verses). There are many explanations offered as to why this piece of land and not some other spot was chosen such as this is where Abraham almost sacrificed Isaac and this is where Jacob had his dream and so on. All of those probably have some validity. But from an economics standpoint, when God says the land would flow with milk and honey, a phrase used to describe the land in four of Moses' five books, He was talking about material prosperity and the first thing that people of that time would know is that through this land several major trade routes passed. A significant reason the land flowed with milk and honey is because the land flowed with trade. The adjacent map shows the ancient Middle Eastern trade routes and several key ones, the King's Highway and the Via Maris, passed through Israel.

The Via Maris, shown as the dotted line in the map, connected to a series of other routes that linked Egypt with the Mesopotamian people and later kingdoms like Assyria, Babylon, and Persia, while the King's Highway, which is mentioned in Numbers 20 and is shown in red extended farther east into Babylon and a large trade network in the Tigris-Euphrates river valley. Israel's geographic advantage continued for centuries. The very wealthy city-states of Tyre, founded in 2750 BC, and Sidon, named after Noah's great-grandson, were on the coast of Israel and were vital trading ports both mentioned in the Old Testament. Caeserea (not shown on the map but near Jaffa), built by Herod the Great, was a vital port in the period before the Roman invasion

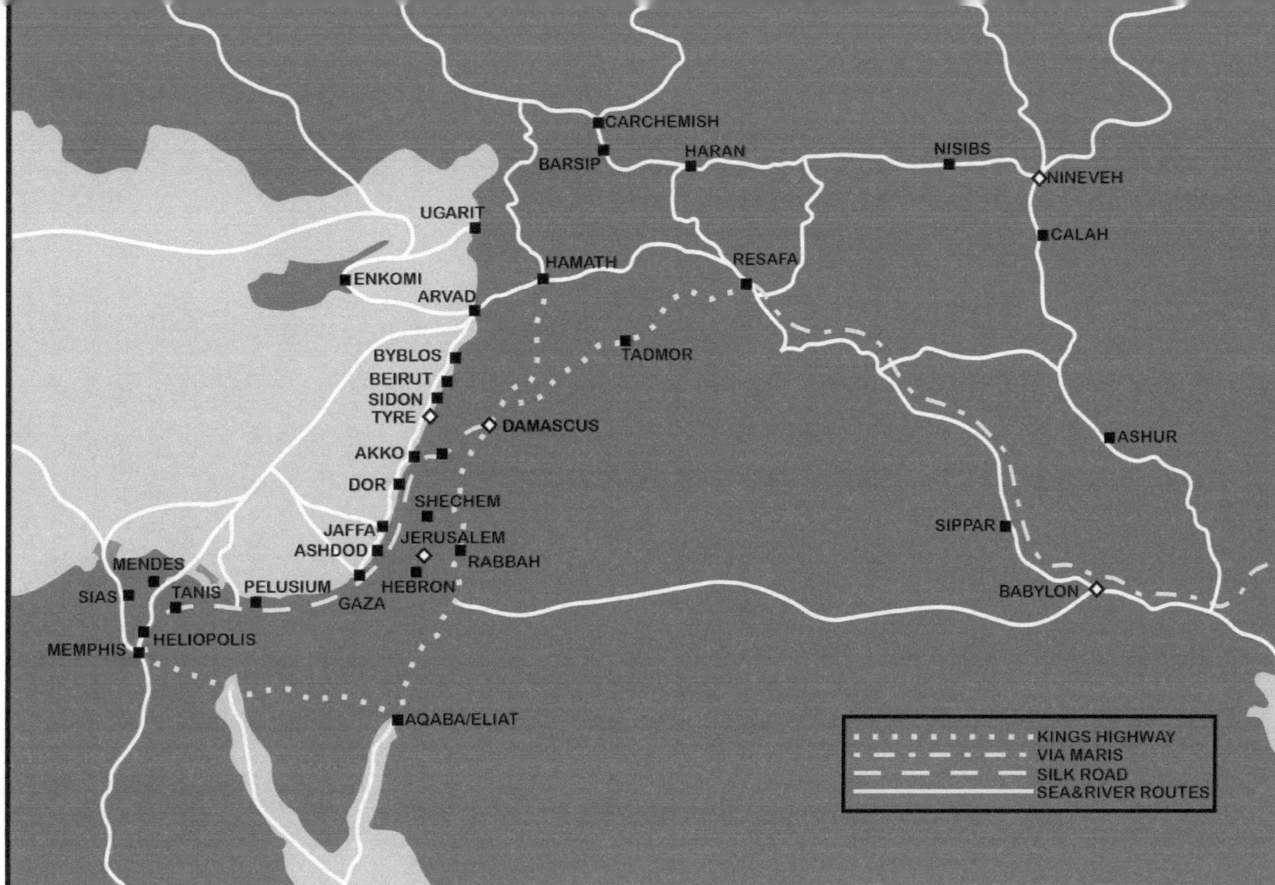


**Figure 7.1. Trade Routes of the Ancient Middle East**
Created by Jeremy D. Schmitz

in 66 AD and even in post-biblical time the region was vital to trade as the Silk Road passed through Damascus and Gaza and Petra (not shown on the map) were part of the trading route that allowed traders to transport far eastern goods to Europe. In short, this area had been vital to trade for thousands of years. It was already vital to trade hundreds of years before the Israelites settled there, it is most likely that Abram used one of these roads to travel to Egypt (Genesis 14) and the Ishmaelites that Joseph's brothers sold him to (Genesis 31) were traveling to Egypt along one of these roads as well. And this area continued to be vital to trade after Israel settled in the area and long after they ceased to exist as a nation. But for a period Israel used its location to become extremely rich for a while.

## ISRAEL'S GOLDEN AGE: THE REIGN OF SOLOMON

The pinnacle of Israel's existence as an independent, self-governing nation was probably during the reign of the third king and the last ruler of the unified kingdom, Solomon. To this day, even among non-believers Solomon is known for his wisdom. In a famous exchange he had with God recorded in 1 Kings 3, God comes to him in a dream and offers Solomon anything he wants and Solomon requests great wisdom so he can rule well and as a result God also grants Solomon wealth, peace, and long life. Solomon wrote three books of the Bible: Proverbs, Ecclesiastes, and Song of Solomon and contributed to the Psalms and he would be fabulously wealthy. The question for our purposes here is, how did he become so wealthy? Well, fortunately the Bible tells us and by its inclusion in this section I am sure you have figured out as well.

One of the first things we learn about Solomon is that he built the temple in Jerusalem: "In the four hundred and eightieth year after the people of Israel came out of the land of Egypt, in the fourth year of Solomon's reign over Israel, in the month of Ziv, which is the second month, he began to build the house of the LORD. The house that King Solomon built for the LORD was 60 cubits long, 20 cubits wide, and 30 cubits high."[7] While there is some debate on exactly how long a cubit is a good approximation is 18 inches or about 46 centimeters, which means the temple would have been 90 feet long (28 meters), 45 feet high (13 meters), and 30 feet wide (9 meters). Not a massive building by today's standards but four and half stories tall with 2,700 square feet (820 meters), a significant undertaking given the technology of the day. In addition to the size of the temple there were to be several rooms and stories within, pillars on the outside and so forth, all of which had significance but is beyond the scope of this discussion which is just to show that it was not just a big stone box and it took seven years to complete.

However, it would have undoubtedly taken much longer had Solomon tried to be self-sufficient and build it with the resources and talent within Israel alone. Something that undoubtedly would appeal to some faithful as he was building the most holy place on the planet, a place that, to the Jewish mind was God's dwelling place on earth, a place that would house the Ark of the Covenant, the original Ten Commandments, and was so holy that there was one part that could only be entered into once a year by only one person in the nation, the high priest. If there was ever a project that should only involve the truest, most faithful, it would be this one. Or not:

> Now Hiram king of Tyre sent his servants to Solomon when he heard that they had anointed him king in place of his father, for Hiram always loved David. And Solomon sent word to Hiram, "You know that David my father could not build a house for the name of the LORD his God because of the warfare with which his enemies surrounded him, until the LORD put them under the soles of his feet. But now the LORD my God has given me rest on every side. There is neither adversary nor misfortune. And so I intend to build a house for the name of the LORD my God, as the LORD said to David my father, 'Your son, whom I will set on your throne in your place, shall build the house for my name.' Now therefore command that cedars of Lebanon be cut for me. And my servants will join your servants, and I will pay you for your servants such wages as you set, for you know that there is no one among us who knows how to cut timber like the Sidonians."
>
> As soon as Hiram heard the words of Solomon, he rejoiced greatly and said, "Blessed be the LORD this day, who has given to David a wise son to be over this great people." And Hiram sent to Solomon, saying, "I have heard the message that you have sent to me. I am ready to do all you desire in the matter of cedar and cypress timber. My servants shall bring it down to the sea from Lebanon, and I will make it into rafts to go by sea to the place you direct. And I will have them broken up there, and you shall receive it. And you shall meet my wishes by providing food for my household." So Hiram supplied Solomon with all the timber of cedar and cypress that he desired, while Solomon gave Hiram 20,000 cors of wheat as food for his household, and 20,000 cors of beaten oil. Solomon gave this to Hiram year by year. And the LORD gave Solomon wisdom, as he promised him. And there was peace between Hiram and Solomon, and the two of them made a treaty.
>
> King Solomon drafted forced labor out of all Israel, and the draft numbered 30,000 men. And he sent them to Lebanon, 10,000 a month in shifts. They would be a month in Lebanon and two months at home. Adoniram was in charge of the draft. Solomon also had 70,000 burden-bearers and 80,000 stonecutters in the hill country, besides Solomon's 3,300 chief officers who were over the work, who had charge of the people who carried on the work. At the king's command they quarried out great, costly stones in order to lay the foundation of the house with dressed stones. So Solomon's builders and Hiram's builders and the men of Gebal did the cutting and prepared the timber and the stone to build the house.[8]

In this passage we see specialization and trade. As a side note we also see the king drafting forced labor that was warned of both in Deuteronomy 17 and 1 Samuel 8 as discussed above, but the focus here is the trade. We need to remember that Tyre was a friend of Israel but they were not part of Israel and would later be subject to a dire prophecy in Ezekiel 26 that saw its fulfillment when Alexander the Great leveled the mainland city and then, using the stones from the destroyed buildings, built a causeway to the harbor island and conquered and razed it too. Its strategic location and unique geography inspired its rebuilding and continued inhabitation and it is now the fourth largest city in Lebanon. However, at this time Hiram and Solomon were friendly and made more so by this very agreeable trading arrangement they entered into where Hiram provided cedars and craftsmen and Solomon provided food (a cor is about 6 bushels). The Bible attributes this trading arrangement to the God-given wisdom Solomon had: "And the LORD gave Solomon wisdom, as he promised him. And there was peace between Hiram and Solomon, and the two of them made a treaty."[9]

This was not the only occasion that Solomon engaged in trade, the evidence points to it being an ongoing activity throughout his entire reign and not just a onetime event to get a special project done. A few chapters later Solomon gets a visit from the Queen of Sheba, a famous event inspiring music, plays, and movies. Tradition and archeological evidence point to Sheba being what is modern-day Ethiopia but there is some disagreement and Sudan, southern Egypt, and even Iran have also been proffered as locations. The point here is not to identify the exact location (Ethiopia seems to make the most sense to me) but to note that all of these are some distance from Israel and the queen probably learned of Solomon from merchants and traders since the passage opens with "Now when the queen of Sheba heard of the fame of Solomon concerning the name of the LORD."[10] As we see from the passage the queen brought a number of items to trade and while seeing Solomon's wealth and meeting him was certainly a goal she fully expected to engage in trade with him as well:

> She came to Jerusalem with a very great retinue, with camels bearing spices and very much gold and precious stones. And when she came to Solomon, she told him all that was on her mind. And Solomon answered all her questions; there was nothing hidden from the king that he could not explain to her . . . And she said to the king, "The report was true that I heard in my own land of your words and of your wisdom, but I did not believe the reports until I came and my own eyes had seen it. And behold, the half was not told me. Your wisdom and prosperity surpass the report that I heard. Happy are your men! Happy are your servants, who continually stand before you and hear your wisdom! Blessed be the LORD your God, who has delighted in you and set you on the throne of Israel!

> Because the LORD loved Israel forever, he has made you king, that you may execute justice and righteousness." Then she gave the king 120 talents of gold, and a very great quantity of spices and precious stones. Never again came such an abundance of spices as these that the queen of Sheba gave to King Solomon.[11]

And Solomon was not just accepting the queen's goods as gift but "King Solomon gave to the queen of Sheba all that she desired, whatever she asked besides what was given her by the bounty of King Solomon."[12] Chapter 10 of first Kings which records the queen's visit explains the source of all this wealth she observed. Solomon is the only Jewish king recorded as having used a trading fleet: "Moreover, the fleet of Hiram, which brought gold from Ophir, brought from Ophir a very great amount of almug wood and precious stones. And the king made of the almug wood supports for the house of the LORD and for the king's house, also lyres and harps for the singers."[13] But Solomon did not just rely on Hiram's fleet. "For the king had a fleet of ships of Tarshish at sea with the fleet of Hiram. Once every three years the fleet of ships of Tarshish used to come bringing gold, silver, ivory, apes, and peacocks. Thus King Solomon excelled all the kings of the earth in riches and in wisdom. And the whole earth sought the presence of Solomon to hear his wisdom, which God had put into his mind. Every one of them brought his presents, articles of silver and gold, garments, myrrh, spices, horses, and mules, so much year by year."[14]

We see that Solomon did not get his wealth through plunder and pillage or as spoils of war but through commerce; "Now the weight of gold that came to Solomon in one year was 666 talents of gold, besides that which came from the explorers and from the business of the merchants, and from all the kings of the west and from the governors of the land." Solomon was trading with Sheba to the south, Hiram to the north and with kings to the west. "And the king made silver as common in Jerusalem as stone, and he made cedar as plentiful as the sycamore of the Shephelah. And Solomon's import of horses was from Egypt and Kue, and the king's traders received them from Kue at a price. A chariot could be imported from Egypt for 600 shekels of silver and a horse for 150, and so through the king's traders they were exported to all the kings of the Hittites and the kings of Syria."[15] It is important to point out that gold and silver are not true wealth, while they are proxy measures in some cases the passage refers to prices and abundance as well as accumulation of precious metals, this was not just a king accumulating shiny metal but reached down to the people and permeated the economy more fully. And so Israel, under Solomon was an active trading nation that was wealthy and importing and exporting to all the nations around it and used its comparative advantages in agriculture and especially having the trade routes to reach the known world with goods and not armies. However, we know this great wealth enticed Solomon to ignore some of the restrictions placed on the king in Deuteronomy, he had many wives, many horses, and much gold, which eventually led to the kingdom splitting after his death. For what we might consider the view for the average person we turn to Proverbs 31 to see a different perspective.

## THE VIRTUOUS WOMAN IS A BUSINESSWOMAN

Proverbs 31 is attributed to Lemuel. We do not confidently know who Lemuel is and there are several theories including that it was another name for Solomon. The name translates as "devoted to God" and may well be a description or possibly a nickname rather than a proper name since the chapter is attributed as having been inspired by the author's mother. It is easy to picture a mother advising a teenage son what to look for in a wife and him reflecting on that advice at some later time, especially Solomon as he ventured far from this advice and suffered for it later in life.

Regardless of who wrote it, it is the Bible's definitive statement on what makes a strong woman and excellent wife. It is worthwhile to examine this, some may be surprised at what they find when looked at a certain way:

> An excellent wife who can find?
> She is far more precious than jewels.
> The heart of her husband trusts in her,
> and he will have no lack of gain.
> She does him good, and not harm,
> all the days of her life.
> She seeks wool and flax,
> and works with willing hands.
> *She is like the ships of the merchant;*
> *she brings her food from afar.*
> She rises while it is yet night
> and provides food for her household
> and portions for her maidens.
> *She considers a field and buys it;*
> *with the fruit of her hands she plants a vineyard.*
> She dresses herself with strength
> and makes her arms strong.
> *She perceives that her merchandise is profitable.*
> Her lamp does not go out at night.
> She puts her hands to the distaff,
> and her hands hold the spindle.
> **She opens her hand to the poor**

**and reaches out her hands to the needy.**
She is not afraid of snow for her household,
for all her household are clothed in scarlet.
She makes bed coverings for herself;
her clothing is fine linen and purple.
Her husband is known in the gates
when he sits among the elders of the land.
*She makes linen garments and sells them;*
*she delivers sashes to the merchant.*
Strength and dignity are her clothing,
and she laughs at the time to come.
She opens her mouth with wisdom,
and the teaching of kindness is on her tongue.
She looks well to the ways of her household
and does not eat the bread of idleness.
Her children rise up and call her blessed;
her husband also, and he praises her:
"Many women have done excellently,
but you surpass them all."
Charm is deceitful, and beauty is vain,
but a woman who fears the LORD is to be praised.
Give her of the fruit of her hands,
and let her works praise her in the gates.[16]

Christian and Jewish girls have been taught these verses for centuries as something to aspire to and one could spend months unpacking all that is here and what it means and what is required to be like this woman. I have added some emphasis in this copy to highlight something many people miss. In asking the average Christian or any random person 'what are the traits of a virtuous woman?' there is a very good chance that being charitable would rank high on the list. That can look many ways, giving money, volunteering time, working for a nonprofit or non-government organization, and so forth. And that is certainly a characteristic as I highlighted in the bolded part. However, with the exception of that verse this entire passage is about a woman who is engaged in business. As Buchanan and Smith observed, "This woman is heavily engaged in trade both locally and 'afar.' She is diligent in home production in order to have something to trade. The wife of Proverbs 31 appears to be a capitalist, and no detractor of globalization in the sense of serving and benefitting from more distant communities through merchants."[17] I highlighted in italics the verses that deal directly with her operating in the marketplace where she sells and buys but almost all the verses deal with that. The use of scarlet and purple were most likely imported clothes or at least dyes, and she is busy producing for the market when she is not at the market.

In addition to that she is investing, buying a field to use to plant a vineyard. If this is a virtuous woman and is an example of virtue in the broader sense then it is largely defined by being active in the marketplace, by engaging in trade to benefit her family and also the poor. She is not just a consumer but as a producer and investor so one can care for one's family, help the poor, and in these activities one serves the Lord and is worthy of praise.

## IS THE CHRISTIAN CHURCH A MARKET?

If the market is God's preferred social order, should we not see its pattern in other places? I think we do. While my focus is Deuteronomy, we have made the occasional side trip, especially in this chapter, and I need to lead us on one more, one that may seem odd and different at first but bear with me. As stated before, the market is where trade and exchange occur and is characterized by people with different specializations in what they do well and producing more than they need and exchanging the surplus with others for goods and services they do not produce so well or at all. We can think of a local farmer's market where the farmer grows much more food than his family will ever eat and takes the surplus to the market to sell to others who do not grow any food. And those customers sell things in their role as a producer of maybe car repair services or economics education, earn income, and use some of it to buy food. While the mechanics can get more complex, this is the basic operation of the market with which we are all familiar if not from study at least from experience.

If we take this analysis and look at the local church, we can see a very similar pattern. I am not saying there is buying and selling going on at a church but there is exchange going on. Christ's sacrifice on the cross was once referred to as the Great Exchange, so the language and concepts are in the Christian tradition. Paul describes the local church in terms of specialization and exchange, just without the price mechanism. In 1 Corinthians 12 Paul compares the church to a human body with Christ as the head:

> Just as a body, though one, has many parts, but all its many parts form one body, so it is with Christ. For we were all baptized by one Spirit so as to form one body—whether Jews or Gentiles, slave or free—and we were all given the one Spirit to drink. Even so the body is not made up of one part but of many.
>
> Now if the foot should say, "Because I am not a hand, I do not belong to the body," it would not for that reason stop being part of the body. And if the ear should say, "Because I am not an eye, I do not belong to the body," it would not for that reason stop being part of the body. If the whole body were an eye, where would the sense of hearing be? If the whole body were an ear, where would the sense of smell be? But in fact God has placed the parts in the body, every one of

> them, just as he wanted them to be. If they were all one part, where would the body be? As it is, there are many parts, but one body.[18]

In an effort to explain to the church at Corinth that all members of the church have a role and are important Paul uses the human body analogy but it also speaks to specialization and exchange. Obviously, the church does not operate like a body all connected to one central nervous system that coordinates all actions, it is composed of different people with different desires and talents and spiritual gifts (as Paul explains later in this same chapter) that must all be coordinated to work together to achieve common goals such as mission work and feeding the poor as well as individual goals such as spiritual growth.

In the market the price system is the coordinating mechanism, we know what we can and cannot do based on the information prices convey to us and that helps us coordinate with whom we will exchange and with whom we will not. The church does not use prices but Paul needs to explain to these early believers that there is a divine coordinating mechanism: "There are different kinds of gifts, but the same Spirit distributes them. There are different kinds of service, but the same Lord. There are different kinds of working, but in all of them and in everyone it is the same God at work. Now to each one the manifestation of the Spirit is given for the common good. . . . All these are the work of one and the same Spirit, and he distributes them to each one, just as he determines."[19] While I certainly cannot say Adam Smith had these verses or even this concept in mind when he described the market system there do seem to be parallels in the logic. Some Corinthians were upset because they were not doing the glamour jobs of preaching and teaching and Paul had to explain how the individual church members worked together as one church sometimes to achieve goals they cannot know or see at the outset, it is in God's hands, hands by the way we cannot see. As Paul was trying to explain how the church works and each member fits and has a role to play, even if it is not a high-profile role, he uses themes of specialization: "If they were all one part, where would the body be? As it is, there are many parts, but one body. The eye cannot say to the hand, 'I don't need you!' And the head cannot say to the feet, 'I don't need you!' On the contrary, those parts of the body that seem to be weaker are indispensable. . . . If they were all one part, where would the body be?"[20]

This is a theme of Paul's not just a onetime explanation for a special case or a particularly troubled church. Paul talks about specialization of the faithful on several occasions. To the very strong church at Rome Paul wrote essentially the same thing:

> For by the grace given to me I say to everyone among you not to think of himself more highly than he ought to think, but to think with sober judgment, each

> according to the measure of faith that God has assigned. For as in one body we have many members, and the members do not all have the same function, so we, though many, are one body in Christ, and individually members one of another. Having gifts that differ according to the grace given to us, let us use them: if prophecy, in proportion to our faith; if service, in our serving; the one who teaches, in his teaching; the one who exhorts, in his exhortation; the one who contributes, in generosity; the one who leads, with zeal; the one who does acts of mercy, with cheerfulness.[21]

However, it was not only Paul that talked about specialization. Peter sounded this theme as well: "Above all, keep loving one another earnestly, since love covers a multitude of sins. Show hospitality to one another without grumbling. As each has received a gift, use it to serve one another, as good stewards of God's varied grace: whoever speaks, as one who speaks oracles of God; whoever serves, as one who serves by the strength that God supplies—in order that in everything God may be glorified through Jesus Christ. To him belong glory and dominion forever and ever. Amen."[22]

Over 1,700 years later, Scottish philosopher Adam Smith echoed some of these same themes. I want to emphasize I am not suggesting that Smith was thinking of these verses nor do I have any evidence to even suggest he was, I am saying there are parallels in his points and Paul's worth analyzing. Smith addressed many topics in his book *An Inquiry into the Nature and Causes of the Wealth of Nations*. It delves into human nature, philosophy, religion, politics, even the debate of the day, American independence. But one of his main goals was to explain what leads to the greatest level of production and what makes people better off, after all that is clearly stated in the title. And he did not waste any time, the opening sentence of the book gets right to the heart of the matter: "[T]he greatest improvement in the productive powers of labor, Division of labor is the great cause of its increased powers, and the greater part of the skill, dexterity, and judgment with which it is anywhere directed, or applied, seem to have been the effects of the division of labor."[23] In other words people have different abilities and dividing the task into parts that reflect those abilities increases production. Smith goes on to give an example of a small pin manufacturer:

> To take an example, therefore, from a very trifling manufacture; but one in which the division of labour has been very often taken notice of, the trade of the pin-maker; a workman not educated to this business (which the division of labour has rendered a distinct trade), nor acquainted with the use of the machinery employed in it (to the invention of which the same division of labour has probably given occasion), could scarce, perhaps, with his utmost industry, make one pin in a day, and certainly could not make twenty. But in the way in which this business is now carried on, not only the whole work is a peculiar

> trade, but it is divided into a number of branches, of which the greater part are likewise peculiar trades. One man draws out the wire, another straights it, a third cuts it, a fourth points it, a fifth grinds it at the top for receiving the head; to make the head requires two or three distinct operations; to put it on, is a peculiar business, to whiten the pins is another; it is even a trade by itself to put them into the paper; and the important business of making a pin is, in this manner, divided into about eighteen distinct operations, which, in some manufactories, are all performed by distinct hands, though in others the same man will sometimes perform two or three of them. I have seen a small manufactory of this kind where ten men only were employed, and where some of them consequently performed two or three distinct operations. But though they were very poor, and therefore but indifferently accommodated with the necessary machinery, they could, when they exerted themselves, make among them about twelve pounds of pins in a day. There are in a pound upwards of four thousand pins of a middling size. Those ten persons, therefore, could make among them upwards of forty-eight thousand pins in a day. Each person, therefore, making a tenth part of forty-eight thousand pins, might be considered as making four thousand eight hundred pins in a day. But if they had all wrought separately and independently, and without any of them having been educated to this peculiar business, they certainly could not each of them have made twenty, perhaps not one pin in a day; that is, certainly, not the two hundred and fortieth, perhaps not the four thousand eight hundredth part of what they are at present capable of performing, in consequence of a proper division and combination of their different operations.[24]

Where one worker, regardless of skills and abilities, may not be able to produce more than twenty pins a day if left to his own devices a small group, organized appropriately, could make thousands all thanks to the division of labor, specialization, and trade in the marketplace.

If we take this analysis and think about Peter and Paul's analogies it is not too much of a stretch to state that the church is a spiritual marketplace where believers with different gifts and abilities can gather to practice good stewardship by exchanging their gifts in serving one another. If division of labor, specialization, and exchange (trade) is the way God organizes His church to accomplish its mission (to maximize evangelism and edification of the saints) then it is safe to assume that this is the way larger society should be organized to maximize its production, as Smith taught us 240 years ago and is still true to this day. We must also remember that in the church market and the commercial market, the goal is to use our talents to the best of our ability to serve others, it is never about chasing profits (spiritual or material) for their own sake. As Jesus tells us about the Pharisees, seeking to be holy in the eyes of others is a losing game, those that play it have their reward already, and Paul says the same about chasing material wealth in 1 Timothy 6. A marketplace is always about using one's talents to their best ability to serve others that is the path to spiritual profits and material profits.

I will close this chapter with an excerpt from a sermon delivered by Martin Luther King Jr. on March 6, 1961, at the Detroit Council of Churches Lenten Services in Detroit, Michigan. In expounding on the encounter Jesus had with a rich ruler in Luke 18 where Jesus tells the man to sell all and follow him, King says the man is foolish because he was self-absorbed and self-focused and did not realize how dependent on others he was. In applying that truth to modern society to show how dependent we all are on each other, King gave a great description of the market system:

> Something should remind us before we can finish eating breakfast in the morning, we are dependent on more than half of the world. We get up in the morning and go to the bathroom and reach over for a sponge, and that's handed to us by a Pacific Islander. Then we reach over for a bar of soap, and that's given to us at the hands of a Frenchman. And then we reach up for our towel, and that's given to us by a Turk. And then we go to the kitchen for breakfast, getting ready to go to work. Maybe this morning we want to follow the good old American tradition, and we drink coffee. That's poured in our cups by a South American or maybe we are desirous of having tea. Then we discover that that's poured in our cup by a Chinese. Or maybe we want cocoa this morning, and then we discover that that's poured in our cup by a West African. Then we reach over for a piece of toast, only to discover that that's given to us at the hands of an English-speaking farmer, not to mention the baker. And so before we finish eating breakfast in the morning, we are dependent on more than half of the world.[25]

In the process of pointing out how dependent we all are on each other, including people we do not know and will never meet, King describes the market system, only leaving out how prices coordinate the process. For another take on this concept I point the reader to Leonard Reed's 1958 essay *I, Pencil*. In pointing out how the rich young ruler was a fool for not understanding how God made us to live in community with each other and how dependent we are on each other, even people we do not know and may never meet, or how the lawyer in Luke 10 who asked Jesus, 'who is my neighbor?' had the same blind spot, King implies we too are fools if we do not understand this reality and that even your simple morning routine should point it out to you. In Romans, Paul tells us that people who look at nature and do not see God are without excuse, His physical order is on display. I think King would agree that God has also put his social order on display as well and when we think about the market system as it works, even imperfectly, we see our connectedness to others is very real, indeed our comfort and frequently our very survival depends on it. Just as God designed.

## NOTES

1. *Proverbs*, n.d., 6:6–8 (ESV).

2. A possibly apocryphal story told around the George Mason University graduate economics program is that one day a professor was walking to the Public Choice Center on campus and ran into Professor Gordon Tullock, who was intently staring at an ant colony. When asked what he was doing, Professor Tullock's one-word reply was "research." There was no indication that he had been reading Proverbs before this incident but there it is, one of the leading Public Choice economists had 'gone to the ant' to learn.

3. "Off-Grid," accessed July 11, 2018, https://www.off-grid.net/.

4. *Genesis*, n.d., 4:2 (ESV).

5. Ibid., 4:20–22 (ESV).

6. Ibid., 37:25–28 (ESV).

7. *1 Kings*, n.d., 6:1–2 (ESV).

8. Ibid., 5 (ESV).

9. Ibid., 5:12 (ESV).

10. Ibid., 10:1 (ESV).

11. Ibid., 10:2–10 (ESV).

12. Ibid., 10:13 (ESV).

13. Ibid., 10:11–12 (ESV).

14. Ibid., 10:22–25 (ESV).

15. Ibid., 10:27–29.

16. *Proverbs*, 31:10–31 (ESV).

17. Arthur Lindsley, ed., *Counting the Cost: Christian Perspectives on Capitalism* (Abilene: Abilene Christian University Press, 2017), P.175.

18. *1 Corinthians*, n.d., 12:12–20.

19. Ibid., 12:4–11 (ESV).

20. Ibid., 12:20–27 (ESV).

21. *Romans*, n.d., 12:3–8 (ESV).

22. *1 Peter*, n.d., 4:8–11 (ESV).

23. Adam Smith, *An Inquiry into the Nature and Causes of the Wealth of Nations by Adam Smith, Edited with an Introduction, Notes, Marginal Summary and an Enlarged Index by Edwin Cannan*, vol. 1 (London: Methuen, 1904), 1.

24. Ibid., 1:2.

25. Martin Luther King Jr., "What Happened to Hell?" (Sermon, Detroit Council of Churches Lenten Services, Detroit, MI, March 6, 1961), http://okra.stanford.edu/transcription/document_images/Vol06Scans/6Mar1961TheManWhoWasaFool,SermonDeliveredattheDetroitCouncilofChurches'NoonLentenServices.pdf.

# *Chapter Eight*

# Culture and Trust, Innovation and Investment

This chapter contains some important issues but none of which seem to merit a whole chapter until themselves, it is sort of a catchall chapter, like that one drawer in the kitchen or your desk that has some important stuff in it but none of which easily fits into the organization scheme of the rest of the room or drawers. The main reason for this is not because these issues are secondary, they are not, and some argue they are primary but, since we are following the Bible's teachings, these issues are not discussed as much. There are principles in scripture that enlighten our thinking on these issues but there is not a "Thus saith the Lord . . . " passage as there is with human dignity or property rights or the limitation on central government. In a sense these are derivative concepts, either naturally occurring for a nation that is following the explicitly stated rules or implied by other rules, customs, and teachings. So, in no particular order I discuss culture and the need for everyday trust, investment and capital, and creativity and innovation.

## CULTURE AND TRUST

When scholars first started thinking about these ideas that we now call economics, topics we now call culture were at the center. Like most every academic discipline, economics began as an extension of theology and philosophy and human interactions were central to those studies. Adam Smith, traditionally recognized as the founder of economics as a discipline, was not an economist, that term did not exist, he was a moral philosopher. Since Smith, the study has been "scientized" primarily made more mathematical. Economists have constructed complex mathematical models trying to understand human behavior. While these models have value and provide insight in many cases they reduce humans to a utility maximizing automaton, only seeking one's own gain, what the economist Deidre McCloskey has nicknamed Max(imum) U(tility). Max U is not a human but merely one narrowly focused side of a human, he would not be a good friend and a horrible boss or spouse. Reducing humans to Max U strips away much of what makes us human in real life; our willingness to sacrifice, to choose a less profitable path so others may prosper, to be charitable, and so forth. It also strips away some of the social cohesion that is absolutely necessary for a functioning society and economy. In the models, some key qualities are just assumed, this is sometimes necessary and useful in order to focus on other aspects but assuming them in a model should never mean forgetting them or their importance. Culture in general and the role of everyday trust in particular fall into that category of assumed and over time forgotten. Some are rediscovering their importance to economic activity and fortunately we see them in the Bible.

After having stated above there is no "Thus saith the Lord . . . " on some of these issues in this chapter, I am going to immediately contradict myself; Deuteronomy does emphasize the need for honesty and truthfulness. "Thou shall not lie." Is very much a "Thus saith the Lord" command and there are extensions of this as well. Deuteronomy 25:15 emphasizes the need for fair weights and measures so that all exchanges are honest, almost all items were paid for by a certain weight of silver or gold that had to be measured out by the merchant as part of the transaction. This command is emphasized and repeated in several places in the Bible as were other specific commands requiring honesty. The interesting aspect to all of this is that many of the examples used deal with contracts and commerce. Besides ten verses that deal with honest weights or punishments for dishonest weights, there are verses about honesty in contracts in both the Old and New Testaments (Genesis 21, 23, and Galatians 3) and I discussed Solomon and Hiram above as well as marriage contracts and the most important of all, the covenant with Israel. All of these come with expectations that both parties have certain obligations and responsibilities they will perform, there is an expectation of honesty and truthfulness and repercussions for failing to meet those obligations and responsibilities.

This expectation for honesty sets a tone for the culture. The Bible emphasizes that oaths, vows, and contracts are very important. So important that in Matthew 5 Jesus tells his listeners in the Sermon on the Mount to let your yes be yes and your no be no and add nothing else to your statements. If you do it may obligate you, to something you cannot do or worse as happened to Peter in his denials of Christ when he denied with an oath and swore he did not know Jesus. He lied and made a vow, expanding his sin as well as putting himself in legal jeopardy had it come to that.

While these are examples of significant events that lead to teachable moments for us and the people then, they point to an important an oft-overlooked concept, the role of everyday trust in economic activity, the weights and measures of everyday life. It is unlikely, although not a certainty, that most readers will not face a Peter moment where your faith or a friend or a strongly held belief seems to be a lifesaving action, a moment when faith and obedience to God meet a very hard test. But, in smaller ways we face these tests every day; will we be honest or cheat? In an analytical tool called game theory there is solution to some games (games just being a term for human interaction that could be competitive or cooperative with different possible outcomes) that is inferior, that is two people engaged in some sort of activity freely agree to an outcome that they both would say they do not want because it makes them worse off, these are called Nash Equilibriums. The primary reason we see such outcomes is because the two parties involved do not trust each other. Think of buying a used car (or anything else). One person wants to buy a car and one wants to sell a car but if the two do not trust each other there will be no sale. There are ways to address this, test drives, money-back guarantees, having the car examined by an independent mechanic, and so forth. These are good and useful but have costs and is certainly not a process we would want to have to go through with every single purchase we make. This would be what we call high transactions costs. If we live in a culture that expects and encourages honesty and truthfulness then we live in a culture in which all sorts of activities are easier to accomplish and less expensive to do. If everyday transactions costs are low then many more transactions can happen, but, it does not take much of a breakdown in everyday trust before an economy will grind to a halt with little trade and little growth. Most people do not think of the many levels and points of trust that occur in everyday activities but those points are plentiful and if we needed to check and inspect and have written contracts at every one nothing would get done. Returning to the used car example, we make jokes about this transaction and many states have Lemon Laws, where a buyer has legal recourse if they are deceptively sold a bad vehicle. But these are all time-consuming and expensive and no one wants to go through that, even the prospect of it is enough to change people's behavior in many cases. Yet we do not end up in these inferior outcomes very often, there is a very active market in used cars. This would not seem to make sense for a Max U person. The incentives in a onetime transaction like selling a used car to someone you do not know is to try to cheat the buyer. The chances of them taking any legal action are slim, the chances that the seller will see the buyer again are slim, and so why not cheat and lie about the car, hide its flaws and issues, and hope they stay hidden for a few weeks and charge the highest price possible based on faulty information? This does happen but not that often. Why not? Well, it is true that the sellers have options, as described before, but there is a prevailing culture of trust in the United States. Some may argue it is breaking down over recent years, and while that may be true, that is a topic for a different book. Right now trust and honesty are still expected because most people tend to be honest and forthright most of the time in their commercial activities. Now, I want to be very clear there is plenty of fraud, corruption, and cheating going on. But in a culture that contains, at least historically, a significant dose of Judeo-Christian ethics and moral code, lying and cheating are still disapproved of and since most people desire to be approved of and accepted and liked there are cultural pressures to not succumb to the temptations of cheating others and be the nastiest Max U one can. If we were all nasty Max Us then we would actually see one of two outcomes; 1) either we would expend large amounts of resources making sure we were not being cheated on all sorts of transactions, we would require contracts and legal assurances and testing and checking and so forth, or 2) our trading network would be very small as we would only trade with people we personally knew to be honest and trustworthy. The world would be full of Nash Equilibriums but they are actually pretty rare.

In his book *Trust* Francis Fukuyama argues that economic prosperity and culture are inseparably connected and that social capital, the quality and quantity of the connections between people, is as important if not more so than physical capital. Fukuyama argues that, what I call a high trust culture, allows for business relations and deals to be more informal, flexible, and therefore easier to form and less costly in terms of time and money. Low trust cultures tend to be more rigid and relationships are harder to form and take more time to form and are most costly in terms of time and money.[1] Take a mental experiment of a simple everyday transaction like buying a loaf of bread. In a high trust culture, a customer walks into a store and buys a loaf of bread and walks out, the whole process takes just a few minutes. But in a low trust culture, and I present an extreme to illustrate a point, there are several decision points in that transaction where trust could break down. Does the retailer trust the producer? Does the customer trust either one? Does the retailer trust the customer? Obviously, there is a sliding scale and no culture is at one extreme or the other but in low trust cultures these questions are addressed by regulations, security measures, detailed contracts with lawyers, and so forth. It is not that the people are inherently less trustworthy than in other places, that may or may not be the case, but they are in a system and culture in which trust is not the norm, it is not practiced enough to be expected, therefore no one else can be relied upon. When this is the case, we tend to see small networks of exchange among people who are related or known to each other and much thinner and weaker networks among people who are more distant, whether that be physically or relationally. All the parties take extra actions when trading outside their known network to ensure they are protected from whatever threats they perceive to exist.

These threats can take many forms in a low trust culture, many of which can be seen even by the casual observer. Even in high trust cultures there are often pockets of low trust neighborhoods where there are more security cameras, alarm systems, bars on windows, merchants who arm themselves and keep the store doors locked to control access. In some countries we see walls and even barbed wire, guards, and dogs. Now these are real but a bit extreme where low trust has manifested itself in physical threats and criminal activity but these are the obvious signs of low trust both in each other and in institutions like the police. But there are many more, if subtler, signs as well.

## DAILY LOW TRUST ISSUES

Maybe more important than the big corruptions of crooked politicians and the like are the daily low trust issues that one has to deal with just to try to get something done. I think some personal examples will illustrate the point of these small signs of low trust that add up and while not easily quantified are costly not only in time and money but also in deteriorating the social capital needed for economic prosperity. The following experiences are true but I omit some details since the point is not to pick on any one country or people but to provide examples of daily low trust issues:

- In one country we visited we had to travel from the capital city where we flew into, to the city where we were staying, 4–5 hours if you can do it at speed. It took us over 7 hours. The reasons for the extra time were related to two factors, both signs of a low trust culture:

  1. It took about an hour of negotiation for our local contact to hire a car and driver.
  2. Every few miles, basically at most every town along the road there was a police checkpoint, which our local friends told us is basically a way for the police to threaten to ticket a driver for any auto infraction . . . unless a little payment can be arranged. We were never actually approached by the police but we had to slow down and wait at every one of these.

- In one country, we visited with some European ex-patriots who had lived in country for several years and we asked them about the differences and the biggest issue they raised was that it was impossible to get a repairman

to come to the house when they said they would. Now this is an issue the world over but their point was not that he would be a few hours late but a few days late if he came at all. That people, including businesspeople who supposedly want business, would lie straight to your face about their intentions has significant impact on the way people operate and plan.
- In another country on a different trip, our driver was stopped. All things considered this turned out pretty well but the situation, which we were ignorant of at the time, involved a driver with no license, a car in violation of several regulations, and speeding. The police work in groups of four or five and one approached the car, left, and a different one returned. She said hello to us and was very friendly and then the driver and officer spoke in a local language for a few minutes and she left and we drove off. Afterward we learned that first officer left because our driver was from a different tribe and the second officer was from the same tribe as our driver and that he had slipped her two separate bribes which we never saw even though we expected it and were looking for it.

Delays and time-consuming negotiations over relatively small transactions, bribery, lying, non-enforcement of rules except for personal gain by officials, and many other daily examples that cost time and money are signals of a low trust culture. The traffic stop experience is particularly insightful as the rules were easily ignored, our driver was only a little concerned when we were stopped. He worked as a hired driver and had no license. Now there can be a worthwhile debate about the nature and need for licensing people for things but that is not the point here, the point is he knew the law was not really enforced and he could bribe any officer that stopped him and pass the cost on to the customer, which he did. And the bribe would be lower and could be negotiated if the officer was a member of his tribe which goes back to the point about low trust cultures being characterized by small networks of exchange, even in bribery, which is just another kind of exchange, people work within their known network.

This leads to other inefficient arrangements such as nepotism. If culture trust is low and it is costly to overcome these knowledge barriers, that is there are few mechanisms to help people build trust in a broader way, then not only will your trade network be smaller and less prosperous than it could be in a high trust culture but a person will make other sub-optimal choices such as hiring only family and friends who may not be the best qualified for a job but you can trust them or at least find them if they break your trust. Of course, hiring and employment are just kinds of exchange so this is merely a sub-category but an important one as we think about the biblical command to be good stewards and how people have different skills and gifts.

In a low trust culture we see poor stewardship as fear dominates thinking and decision making and resources are expended on protection and not production and exchange networks are small and limited. This is not the path to prosperity and flourishing.

Deuteronomy expects a high trust culture. Honesty and truthfulness are emphasized in the Ten Commandments. But we can see this in explicit commands beyond the Ten Commandments as well such as the requirement that judges be unbiased, and not respect rank or position and not take bribes and the previously discussed command to use fair weights and measures. But there are also implicit and probably just as strong elements of trust in the Deuteronomy system. First of all, the entire society is based on faith. Any society based on faith in a God that has no physical manifestation and strictly commands that no such manifestation be made, requires a large element of trust. There are large elements of trust (in this sense I am using faith and trust interchangeably) in the sacrifice system, I will examine the sacrifice system in more detail below, but the people trusted that God remembered his promises to forgive their sins and one day send a Messiah. Second, the nation was placed on the trade routes and expected to be active traders and lenders to the nations. These are business deals with very extended networks. Not only were they working outside their tribes but outside their country with people who not only spoke a different language but had an entirely different religion and culture. Solomon, already discussed in great detail above, made deals with others from all over the map. Thirdly, there was a historical aspect. Abraham, the father of the Jewish people and faith, demonstrated his trust in God and his promises over and over again. Not flawlessly, but certainly with a faithfulness that set the tone for what it meant to be Jewish. He traded with the Hittites and the Egyptians and others and was a significant presence wherever he went, respected because he usually was honest in his dealings, even insisting on paying when it seemed to not be expected.

Culture manifests in many ways; religion, history, art, language, festivals, holidays, even legends and myths are all part of a people's culture. There are many variations and it makes the world a rich and interesting place and one reason travel can be so rewarding. But, all these issues aside, if a culture is a low trust culture and people do not trust each other and institutions such as police and courts are not reliable then there will be daily costs and inconveniences that slow commerce and requires expending time and money then a nation, or more accurately people, will not prosper. A nation may be full of natural resources and hardworking people with ideas and goals, but if it takes bribes to start a business and markets are limited to whom you know and trust, it will be like making a world-class sprinter run in deep mud, all that potential is lost and wasted on just getting through the muck.

## ENTREPRENEURSHIP AND INNOVATION

Deuteronomy says almost nothing on this topic directly and yet it implies a great deal. First, we must have a good definition of entrepreneurship. It is common to assume that anyone who starts a business or some organization is an entrepreneur and while many business operators are entrepreneurial-minded, not all are, there are distinctions in these definitions and some business operators are not entrepreneurs and some entrepreneurs do not start a business or organization. More than starting a business, the two key factors of being an entrepreneur are alertness and creativity, seeing a problem and proposing a solution. It may be a problem no one else sees or knows exists and the person who sees the problem and solution may not be in a position to take action. This is an important distinction because alertness and creativity are innate while taking action often depends on circumstances. We can think of the entrepreneur's alertness as seeing chaos or disorder where others see order and seeing a solution when others do not even see the problem.

A person who starts a business may not really be entrepreneurially minded, he may sell products already on the market using marketing and management methods others are already using. His sole contribution may be seeing the opportunity to serve a currently unserved market, which is no small thing and quite valuable, but even that bit of information may have come to him from someone else. It is easy to imagine a scene where two people are walking down the street and one says this neighborhood really needs an office supply store (or whatever) and the other person agrees and acts on it. The first person really had the entrepreneurial moment, he saw a need and a solution, the second person was a risk taker and had a vision on how to act but not the initial insight. That is the distinctive quality of an entrepreneur, to have a vision for what could be, which is what happens when creativity and alertness mix. We must keep in mind that really what this vision or insight is, is seeing a way to serve other people better, a very Judeo-Christian impulse. Maybe it is no accident that one of the leading scholars on entrepreneurship is also a Jewish rabbi, Dr. Israel Kirzner, who sums this idea up nicely: "[T]he pure entrepreneur . . . is a decision-maker whose entire role arises out of his alertness to hitherto unnoticed opportunities."[2]

But the question remains, if the Bible does not directly address entrepreneurship, even with this richer definition, does entrepreneurship really fit into God's created order? Well, yes. And it starts in Genesis 1:1 when the first thing the Bible tells us is that God is a creator: "In the beginning God created . . . "[3] Not too long after this opening verse, it states that man was made in His image, which implies that man is also a creator. That should not be a surprise, the world is full of art and music and literature and poetry and many other creative works, the only new part is considering work in the commercial space as creative. It is not stretching the point to claim that starting a profit-seeking enterprise is a creative act along the same lines as composing music or writing a poem?

To answer that question, we need to take a closer look at the original creation story to truly understand the Bible's idea of creation. In the Genesis story, God creates the universe out of nothing and after that first phase of creation, the earth is called *tohu* and *vavohu* in the Hebrew (וָבֹהוּ תֹהוּ). This is often translated to some version of formless and empty; the King James Version uses the more poetic "void and without form" but some other English translations are "void and empty," and "waste and void." However, translation, especially of ancient languages, is greatly dependent on context. These words, or forms of them, are used in other parts of the Bible have been translated as waste or laid waste, desert, emptiness, vanity, nothing, and chaos. All these terms convey a strong meaning but I particularly like the term *chaos*. It implies that what existed before God finished creation was not some sort of peaceful, serene existence where God and the angels were just sort of lounging about. You could get that idea from the translation nothingness. Sometimes we like nothingness. If you have a long day, a hard day with people pulling at you in all directions and you feel like you are fighting a hundred fires at a time and up against all the deadlines and you finally come home and it is quiet and peaceful and no one's demanding your time or your energies, then nothingness can be nice. But chaos is never nice or pleasant. It needs to be tamed and controlled. God brought order to this chaos through the rest of his creative activity.

This theme of moving from chaos or at least a lower order to a higher order extends beyond the creation story. In reality it is one of the main themes in the Bible. The Jewish people went from slavery through the wilderness to the Promised Land, the Bible tells us that the arc of time starts in a garden that needed tended and cared for and ends in a new city and notes that the same trees appear in both places implying the city is replacing the garden as a better arrangement. Jesus calms the angry sea, Elijah hears God's voice in a calming whisper after the earthquake, fire, and whirlwind, and of course we have the direct statement from Paul, "For God is not a God of confusion but of peace."[4] The word *confusion* is sometimes translated disorder and the word frequently translated as peace is *shalom* and that is an important concept in understanding the biblical nature of entrepreneurship.

Now, with that as background and remembering we are created in His image as creators, we should see the creative act more expansively then art and literature, they are merely sub-fields of the broader concept of bringing order out of chaos or value out of the valueless. Blank paper and pen in the right hands becomes *Hamlet* (Shakespeare), the *Fifth Symphony* (Beethoven), or *Guernica* (Picasso), creations worth millions of dollars that have brought untold entertainment and education to generations over the decades. But that same paper and pen can also become the plans for a new computer, production process, or market strategy that can also be worth millions and bring untold value to generations. Far too often people overlook creativity in the commercial sphere but they are acts that bring order out of chaos and value out of the valueless.

Professor Kirzner proposes the idea that one significant role entrepreneurs fill is that they find a way to use resources more effectively. They have the same resources and time as everyone else but discover a better way to use them. This mirrors two important biblical concepts: *shalom* and stewardship.

As discussed previously, *shalom* is frequently translated peace but that is not a complete translation. A more complete translation of the term is the flourishing that occurs when all things work together as God intended, it is a more holistic concept than the absence of violence or strife. We can think of the world bumbling its way along with things being forced together and not fitting together or working very well from which conflict and even violence arises. The absence of violence does not necessarily mean we are working together better, it may just mean we stopped trying or learned to live with a bad fit. Entrepreneurs, in their role of finding better ways to use resources, move this imperfect world toward better coordination, a better fit, and greater flourishing. They do not just reduce violence but provide a way for some parts to work together and in so doing bring a little *shalom* to some part of the world.

The second concept is stewardship. So often stewardship is reduced to narrower applications such as money management or environmental issues, but the term *steward* comes from the same root Greek word, *oikonomia*, from which we get the term *economy* and that word properly translated means household manager. A steward is one who manages the resources with which he has been entrusted and as we know from Jesus' parable of the three stewards in Matthew 25 (or Luke 19) that does not mean burying your talents (resources) in the ground. Preservation is not proper stewardship (a lesson for the environmentally minded but I digress). Productive use is proper stewardship.

Entrepreneurs provide ways for better stewardship. A brief historical example may be useful here. In the nineteenth century the primary fuel for lighting was whale oil. Entire local economies such as Mystic, Connecticut, were built around whaling fleets and the whales were hunted mercilessly. Unlike cattle there is no way to domesticate and raise whales so that created some very bad incentives and some very bad outcomes for the whale populations. Meanwhile all over Pennsylvania, Texas, Oklahoma, and other places, there was this black goo oozing out of the ground that some used as bug repellant but otherwise was going largely unused and viewed as a nuisance since it ruined farmland. While oil had been used here and there in history for lamp fuel, it was the refining process that really pushed the process forward. In 1849 the process to distill kerosene from crude oil was invented and by 1857 whale oil was pretty much gone from the market and in 1859 the first American oil well was drilled in Titusville, Pennsylvania (there had been some already drilled in Poland and Canada a few years earlier). In 1878 Edison had invented the light bulb which sent the oil industry into a recession as electricity was far better than kerosene for lighting just as kerosene has been far better than whale oil. Each entrepreneur, using resources that had always been available, found ways to practice better stewardship and bring greater *shalom* to the world in many ways, including ways that they had no intention to impact such as saving the whale populations.

You may still be questioning if a profit-seeking enterprise can really serve God's purposes, businesses are about profits and frequently accused of being only about profits and for putting profits over people while the faithful are commanded to serve God and serve others. But we need to dispel some myths and misconceptions and think more seriously about what entrepreneurs actually do and how the successful ones get that way.

When Jesus was asked, "what is the greatest commandment?" he answered by quoting a passage in Deuteronomy "Hear, O Israel: The LORD our God, the LORD is one. You shall love the LORD your God with all your heart and with all your soul and with all your might" and summarizing another concept "love your neighbor as thyself."[5] We saw in Proverbs 31 and with the Good Samaritan some ways we love others, by meeting the needs of the hurt and poor, but charity is not the main way we serve others. The main way we serve other is through business. That will sound pretty controversial to some who may think that profits and mission should not and really cannot mix, after all we cannot serve two masters, but that is the wrong way to look at this idea.

While there are many differences between the times of ancient Israel and today, one thing is the same and true in both eras and all the ones in between; the average person spends much more time working than worshiping. Depending on denominational practices the most faithful may spend as much as ten hours a week in church-related activities and most of that would be in worship activity not serving others in the sense of meeting their physical needs. The sort of work like that, volunteering at a soup kitchen and such, may not amount to ten hours a month. Yet we spend many hours working every week. If our only way to serve others is in acts of charity, then most of us are not doing very much or very well, most of us just do not have the time. We may give money and help in other ways and that is good as far as it goes but that is not the sort of personal hands-on service that is characterized by the example of the Good Samaritan. But the Good Samaritan model is not the main way we serve each other if by serve we mean meet other people's needs.

The fact is that business and commercial activity is the primary way we serve each other. We get our food, our housing, our clothing, and most everything else from others brought together through the market system to serve us, as Martin Luther King Jr. so aptly explained in his sermon quoted in the previous chapter. In turn that is how we serve others as well. The role entrepreneurs play in all of this is by discovering the best ways we can serve one another and then making that available to the rest of us to either serve in their new system or be served by their new system. Entrepreneurs may be the most attuned to what people need, far more so than charities. Charities respond to needs they clearly see and that is good but entrepreneurs in many cases anticipate needs people do not even know they have. Frequently using resources people thought a nuisance (like oil), entrepreneurs have to be very "otherly" minded, alert to people's future needs, and creative enough to figure out how to meet those needs effectively. They are the epitome of stewardship and creativity and if they fail, they bear all the risk and cost. Those that criticize earning profits and see businesses as greedy institutions that supposedly put profits over people, miss the fact that in a market system, such as the Bible prescribes and as all wealthy countries have in some version however imperfect, it is impossible to put profits over people, people are the source of profits, they are the reason businesses exist. Profits are just the tangible measure that a business has effectively identified a need (looked to others first), and effectively met it (used creativity and practiced good stewardship).[6]

## INVESTMENT AND CAPITAL FORMATION

There are two misconceptions I need to address before getting into this subject fully. The first is the role of capital in growth and development. Capital has been the driving engine of development theory and policy for decades. The neo-classical growth models emphasize capital and differences in capital as a major explanatory factor between wealthy and poor countries. This thinking was behind the idea (oversimplified here) that if wealthy nations give enough money to poor ones, they will eventually be wealthy too. Logic and experience show that capital differences alone are not good in explaining how and why nations become wealthy. Logically, if we examine the history of wealthy countries they were not always endowed with capital. Every wealthy country started poor, it is not like the inhabitants woke up one morning to find by some miracle they were blessed with farm equipment, buildings, and so forth, and suddenly they had capital and no one else did. Capital has to be developed and that is often a long and arduous process. To believe that capital is a major cause for the differences between rich and poor countries largely depends on the historical starting point for the analysis. This project is to determine how a country can go from slavery to prosperity using ancient Israel and Deuteronomy as a model. Modern Israel is relatively wealthy having a per capita GDP about the same as Spain or Italy and they have more capital then poorer countries but that tells us about the situation today, not how it happened. We are starting at the beginning when Israel had no capital.

The other misconception I need to address, is to say capital has no importance at all which some biblical scholars claim for ancient Israel. They look at Deuteronomy 23:19–20 (and some related verses in Leviticus) and see a very clear "thus saith the Lord": "You shall not charge interest on loans to your brother, interest on money, interest on food, interest on anything that is lent for interest. You may charge a foreigner interest, but you may not charge your brother interest, that the LORD your God may bless you in all that you undertake in the land that you are entering to take possession of it."[7] Loans with interest, which is the heart of modern banking and significant in capital formation and investment activity, are forbidden, after all banking, based on these verses, was officially forbidden for Christians in Europe for hundreds of years, although Rodney Stark (see Appendix A for biography) makes the case that this prohibition was not widely enforced.[8] But the question I need to explore is, was lending with interest and at least some sort of proto-banking truly forbidden in Deuteronomy and ancient Israel? And what was the general attitude toward capital formation?

## BIBLICAL LENDING

There are three basic aspects to lending in the modern banking system: the loan, the collateral, and the interest. Lending is clearly not forbidden. The passage talks about not charging interest for a loan, so making a loan was acceptable as was lending to surrounding nations, which was actually encouraged. There are a number of verses, even in the next chapter, that lay out rules about lending. And carrying over in the New Testament Jesus actually tells parables about lending such as in Matthew 25. So, it is clear that making and taking loans was not forbidden and common enough that it needs to be addressed in the law.

It is also true that lending with collateral was acceptable as Deuteronomy 24 discusses how to handle a borrower's pledge against a loan:

"No one shall take a mill or an upper millstone in pledge, for that would be taking a life in pledge . . . " When you make your neighbor a loan of any sort, you shall not go into his house to collect his pledge. You shall stand outside, and the man to whom you make the loan shall bring the pledge out to you. And if he is a poor man, you shall not sleep in his pledge. You shall restore to him the pledge as the sun sets, that he may sleep in his cloak and bless you. And it shall be righteousness for you before the LORD your God.[9]

The point here not being what these rules imply (but respect for property and people are embedded in this) but that collateral (pledge) for a loan was appropriate and acceptable but there were some rules about how it worked.

This brings us to interest which is the most controversial part of the discussion but it is a more nuanced discussion than it first appears. Many of the verses dealing with usury link it to being unjust to the poor. Exodus 22:25 addresses interest in the context of lending to the poor: "If you lend money to any of my people with you who is poor, you shall not be like a moneylender to him, and you shall not exact interest from him."[10] and in Leviticus it states, "If your brother becomes poor and cannot maintain himself with you, you shall support him as though he were a stranger and a sojourner, and he shall live with you. Take no interest from him or profit, but fear your God, that your brother may live beside you. You shall not lend him your money at interest, nor give him your food for profit."[11] Both of these verses tie the prohibition to interest to assisting the poor. The Exodus verse implies there are money lenders and there is no universal condemnation of them and the Exodus verses prohibit charging interest and profiting from selling food, which is not prohibited anywhere else. We see the same idea in passages after Deuteronomy as well. In Ezekiel it lumps charging interest in with a number of serious violations:

If he fathers a son who is violent, a shedder of blood, who does any of these things (though he himself did none of these things), who even eats upon the mountains, defiles his neighbor's wife, oppresses the poor and needy, commits robbery, does not restore the pledge, lifts up his eyes to the idols, commits abomination, lends at interest, and takes profit; shall he then live? He shall not live. He has done all these abominations; he shall surely die; his blood shall be upon himself.[12]

This verse does not directly state the violation on usury is tied to poverty alleviation but it includes failing to restore a pledge as an offense as is oppressing the needy.

Furthermore, it was acceptable to lend with interest to foreigners so if usury were a sin it would be universally forbidden as is theft, murder, and so forth and that is not the case at all. Plus, in the New Testament, Jesus emphasizes the acceptance of interest in his parable about the three stewards the master left with talents to care for. As mentioned before, Jesus puts the traveling master in the role of God the Father who admonishes the unfaithful steward: "But his master answered him, 'You wicked and slothful servant! You knew that I reap where I have not sown and gather where I scattered no seed? Then you ought to have invested my money with the bankers, and at my coming I should have received what was my own with interest.'"[13] As a side note, we see the master reaps where he does not sow and gathers where he has no scattered, which is another way to say he engages in trade, he is a merchant or a broker who is buying and selling products he has not produced. But the main point here is that Matthew, a Jewish writer writing for a Jewish audience about a parable the Jewish Messiah and rabbi told, had God the Father encourage a servant to deposit his money with the bank. While the passage in Deuteronomy is not explicit, taking the other passages that deal with the subject it seems that the ban on usury is connected to helping the poor and not a universal ban on all interest in all circumstances. This is how Calvin and some of the other Reformers read the verse as well. However, there is more to examine than the verses on usury.

## THE INVESTMENT MINDSET

Maybe more than a law on usury and an institutional process, investment and capital formation is a mindset. It requires a willingness to forgo current consumption and a faith that the future will be better as a result. The unfaithful steward in Matthew 25 had institutions available to at least earn some interest, if not the 100 percent return his colleagues earned, but his mindset was all wrong. He was fearful and too focused on the present and missed the potential longer-run gains that were available. The backdrop to much of the Bible is about current sacrifice for greater returns in the long run. Many of these returns are spiritual in nature but the idea of making sacrifices today, deferring current pleasure and consumption for greater pleasures and consumption opportunities in the future, is a constant theme from Genesis to Revelation and for a people who took their faith seriously this would send a clear message and create a distinct mindset not only in the spiritual realm but in the temporal one as well.

One of my favorite examples of this mindset, of making a sacrifice in the present for a future return, what we call in one word an investment, is one of the subtlest examples and is easily missed. In Genesis 21, after Isaac was born, God reiterated His promise to Abraham that one day, 400 years hence, Abraham's children would live in this land. At the end of the chapter there is a little, easily missed verse: "Abraham planted a tamarisk tree in Beersheba and called there on the name of the Lord, the Everlasting God."[14] Why did Abraham do this? Why should we care that he planted a tree or possibly a grove of trees? It is the kind of verse the reader is likely to move past to get to the important stuff. But why is this verse here and what does it tell us? Quite a bit. Planting the tree was an act of faith, earlier Abraham had built a well in this area which of course has immediate use and long-term use but trees take a long time to grow and the tamarisk tree takes a very long time, several hundred years to mature in that harsh climate. By planting this tree, which would undoubtedly reproduce over time and create a shady grove around his well, Abraham was expressing his trust in God's promise by investing in an improvement project he would never be able to utilize. But his descendants would and those trees would be there waiting for them marking the well and providing some shade when they got there a few centuries later. Abraham had faith in God's promise and what the future would look like and made a long-term real investment in that future.

Another mindset lesson was found in one of the core aspects of ancient Judaism: the sacrifice system. The sacrifice system predates Abraham, as discussed in a previous chapter Cain and Abel practiced it as did Noah and presumably others. The system is full of spiritual significance about the forgiveness of sins and foretelling of the Messiah to come and His act as a substitute for a fallen people. However, not to diminish the spiritual significance of this important act, it also reinforces the idea that forgoing some current consumption can have positive long-term benefits. For a people who clearly connected the spiritual to the temporal it is not a stretch to say that the sacrifice system mirrors the investment act. As Jordan Peterson insightfully points out, "When engaging in a sacrifice, our forefathers began to act out what would be considered a proposition . . . *that something better might be attained in the future by giving up something of value in the present*" (emphasis in the original).[15]

The sacrifice system teaches that giving up something of value now leads to a better future, it ensures spiritual prosperity pleasing the Lord, if done in the right spirit and with the right heart. It is a small jump to applying that to other areas of life.

Do we have any reason to believe this theoretical connection is accurate? Again, the evidence is circumstantial but strong. Maybe the strongest evidence is the fact that there were cities throughout Israel. These were not large by any standard, Jerusalem may have never exceeded 100,000 residents even at its highest (although estimates vary quite a bit from 20,000 to 250,000), but they did exist, by some record Israel had more than forty named and notable cities during its kingdom period. Regardless of how many it was they established cities. It is true some were already built and the Israelites just occupied them, but even those require upkeep and maintenance. This is so obvious we do not even think about what it means, it means both physical infrastructure like roads, buildings, and in those days walls and gates and social infrastructure like a city management system. Significant portions of the physical infrastructure they built is still present today. This is a significant investment, some economists have asked the simple but deceptively complex question of why one generation builds anything that will outlast it. What is it that people derive from building anything, a building, road, bridge, or an intangible like a family dynasty or organization that will last longer than they will live? In some places this is not the case, the average house in Japan loses all value, fully depreciates in twenty-two years.[16] But this was not the Jewish approach, the ban on usury, which probably did not preclude actual banking, certainly did not preclude other investment activity. The Jewish people had an investment mindset which may have come from lessons learned from the sacrifice system but regardless of where it came from, the evidence for it is quite abundant in almost every archeological excavation in the country.

## THE EVIDENCE FROM THE OLIVE OIL INDUSTRY

Beyond the mindset created by the sacrifice system and the evidence from archeology we can look at some other evidence. The nature of being an agrarian culture also provides an investment mindset. Waiting for crops to grow and ripen, turning olives into olive oil, which was a very significant part of the Israel economy, and grapes into wine are just a few indications of the understanding of investing. Olive oil may be the most interesting to explore. It involved quite a bit of capital to be successful producing olive oil. Olives grow on trees which are naturally slow-growing, depending on the species three to twelve years before the first fruit appears. Trees require significant space and, relative to other plants, more water. Then, once the olives were harvested, they had to be crushed by a gethsemane. Many Christians think of Jesus' last night spent in the Garden of Gethsemane not realizing that it was a sort of a factory where olives were turned in oil. Some processed the olives outside but the better ones put the crushing floor in a large room, maybe a cave, large enough for several people, animals, and several pieces of equipment. The centerpiece was usually a large round stone that lay in circular trough. This was the gethsemane. It was turned by a donkey or ox (or people) walking in circles to crush the olives into a paste. The paste was put into baskets and taken to another machine that would crush the paste under large weights which would be increased over several days and that process would squeeze oil out of the paste. This process involved a significant amount of specialized equipment that had to be built in a sizable and specialized facility. Jesus and the disciples were in the Garden of Gethsemane because owners would sometimes rent out the space to overnight visitors when olives were not in season.

I am not claiming Israel was unique in its understanding of the investment mindset and the advantages of investing. Many nations built cities, had capital intensive agriculture, and sacrificed to gods. Many cultures grasped the idea that forgoing some consumption today and using it in certain ways may bring better results later. There are many ways to analyze the investment activity of a culture but we should not be put off by the usury issue and the interpretation some have given it over the years. Israel was obviously investing, developing specialized capital, and understood the structure of production. However, there is one unique aspect of Israel and it is an important one that I want to conclude this chapter with, because it is a problem that plagues the developing world; ancient Israel did not waste resources on monuments to their own greatness or any other expensive public work. Probably due to the prohibition on idol making and idol worship and the fact that they never considered their kings as gods or their priests as kings, there is little in the way of unproductive capital. Israel did not construct tomb complexes for their kings, or ziggurats, and or any wonder of the ancient world. Its one public work, the temple, was relatively modest compared to the Parthenon or to the temple to Diana at Ephesus. It is true that Herod the Great, a non-Jew, Rome-installed king left some buildings and monuments to himself such as the Herodian and Masada but for ancient Israel when Deuteronomy was fully in effect as the political-economic organizing document the traces of their past culture are far more likely to be found in the remnants of commerce such as oil presses and faith such as the Western Wall, which itself was probably built by Herod but was an expansion of Nehemiah's temple from five hundred years earlier. One reason archeology is more difficult and information on ancient Israel is so sparse is that they spent little time and resources on such self-important edifices. Many religious Jews and Christians would say the Judeo-Christian faith and culture is the most important legacy, not an earthly structure, and one need not look any further than the faith traditions of close to two billion people to see the true returns on investment.

## NOTES

1. Francis Fukuyama, *Trust: The Social Virtues and the Creation of Prosperity* (New York: Free Press, 1995).
2. Israel M. Kirzner, *Competition and Entrepreneurship*, 7. Dr (Chicago: Univ. of Chicago Press, 1993), 39.

3. *Genesis*, n.d., 1:1 (ESV).
4. *1 Corinthians*, n.d., 14:33a (ESV).
5. *Matthew*, n.d., 22:35–40 (excerpts) (ESV).
6. This fact does not really fit the flow of the chapter but it is of significance when we talk about ideas and innovation and creativity. Since its inception the Nobel Prize has been awarded to 923 people and organizations (through 2017). Over 200 times or 22.5 percent of the awards have been to Jewish recipients. Less than one percent of the world's population is Jewish which means that Jewish winners have exceeded expectations along a magnitude of 11,250 percent. As we discuss culture and creativity in these last two sections, it is worth noting that a culture that looks to Deuteronomy as its founding document has had incredible success at the highest levels of intellectual achievement and creativity and while any achievement like this has many contributing factors, one is a strong cultural foundation that esteems creativity all the more remarkable in remembering that the Jewish people had no geographical home from 66–1948.
7. *Deuteronomy*, n.d., 23:19–20 (ESV).
8. Rodney Stark, *The Victory of Reason: How Christianity Led to Freedom, Capitalism, and Western Success*, Random House trade pbk. ed (New York: Random House Trade Paperbacks, 2006).
9. *Deuteronomy*, 24:6, 10 (ESV).
10. *Exodus*, n.d., 22:25 (ESV).
11. *Leviticus*, n.d., 25:35–37 (ESV).
12. *Ezekiel*, n.d., 18:12–13 (ESV).
13. *Matthew*, 25:26–27 (ESV).
14. *Genesis*, 21:33.
15. Jordan B. Peterson, *12 Rules for Life: An Antidote to Chaos* (London: Allen Lane, 2018), 164.
16. "Why Japanese Houses Have Such Limited Lifespans," *The Economist*, n.d., https://www.economist.com/finance-and-economics/2018/03/15/why-japanese-houses-have-such-limited-lifespans.

# *Part 3*

# CONCLUSION

## "How Then Should We Live?"

I take the title of this chapter from one of Francis Schaeffer's (see Appendix A for biography) most popular works. It is the ending of a larger question Schaeffer implicitly asked and answered: if all of this (the Bible) is true, "how then should we live?" In Schaeffer's case he was dealing with the arc of the history and theology of philosophy, science, and religion. It is a significant work worth the time to read. I am dealing merely with economics and the commercial life of a people and how they can flourish, but the question is still appropriate. If I have presented what Schaeffer may have called true truth about the path to flourishing, then what is to be done?[1]

This is not a typical economics book, as you well know by now. It is not full of graphs, equations, and curves. While I included a few statistics, I do not rely on traditional economic measures to make my case. This book is not intended for a professional economics audience. I have two audiences for this book; first, Christians everywhere, but especially in the West, who want to understand what the Bible says about economics, and, second, Christians in the developing world looking for support on how their economies can flourish. I think both groups suffer from the same issue, they look at the modern West and see something called capitalism, a word I rarely use, and see cronyism, bailouts, corruption, heavy regulations, a tax code riddled with favoritism, and plenty of other flaws and problems and rightly wonder if it is moral and proper and biblical. I am here to say just like churches, families, and marriages that are also flawed and have their problems and do not follow the Bible model perfectly, the market economy, flaws and all, in its implementation is what the Bible prescribes. It is our job to fix it where we can and how we can, but to dismiss it and replace with some man-made centralized system would be a tragic mistake . . . of biblical proportions.

## MODERN ECONOMICS MISSES THE POINT

In another sense my ultimate audience is not either of these groups but people who will probably never read it but are epitomized in a story that the respected Chilean economist Manfred Max-Neef (see Appendix A for biography) tells in his book *Outside Looking In: Experiences in Barefoot Economics* but also told to me personally when I visited with him in 2007. It sums up the problem modern economics faces; Max-Neef says he was in an Indian village in the Sierra in Peru on a rainy, nasty, ugly day and found himself standing across from a villager, a man with a large extended family depending on him but who had no work and limited prospects. Max-Neef said as he looked as this villager and considered his situation and realized that he, with all his education and knowledge, had nothing useful or helpful to say to this man in his circumstances, that his language as an economist was useless. That telling this man that Peru's GDP was up 5 percent was not useful, maybe even insulting. Max-Neef says it was then he realized that modern economics was woefully inadequate to address real poverty where it is.[2] Others, like Deidre N. McCloskey, who may well find herself on the other side of Max-Neef on many issues, have reached the same conclusion as McCloskey tells us in the title of the first volume of her wonderful trilogy *Bourgeois Dignity: Why Economics Can't Explain the Modern World.*

Both economists have captured in their own work a truth that modern economics has lost its foundational roots. It sees itself as part of an inner sanctum, being in and close to power making and advising on policy with very little concern in actually educating people and explaining how we become prosperous. An example may make the point better.

Professor Jonathan Gruber is a highly respected health care economist at the Massachusetts Institute of Technology (MIT). He has been there since 1992 and sits on a number of committees and edits journals and has generally achieved great success in his career. This got him selected to be part of the team that designed the Affordable Care Act under President Obama. Professor Gruber got into some trouble by stating not once, but on four different occasions that we know of, that the Obama administration was able to pass the legislation because the American voter is economically stupid.[3] I have provided some links in the endnote but it is easy to find on YouTube. He may not represent the profession's thinking but he is not alone, although he may be the only one to say it in polite company and on the record. While it says something about him and the American people's level of economics understanding, it really says the most about economics instructors. Few people are born innately understanding economics, if the profession has not found a way to make the subject interesting enough for people to at least learn the basics then that is not the people's fault. There is evidence people are interested; when the material is presented in a lively and interesting way people buy books, watch shows, and listen to podcasts. So, to the extent that anyone complains this is not a typical economics book, I respond that is a feature not a bug.[4]

In addition to not being full of charts and equations, this is a book that takes the Bible seriously. Old ideas, especially religious ones, tend to be dismissed by modern thinkers, the pressure in modern academia is to find the new and cutting edge, defending the old is a career stopper but as Max-Neef, McCloskey, and others have pointed out, modern ideas do not seem to be answering age-old questions very well. Even if one were to dismiss the spiritual and miraculous from the Bible, it is an enduring book where people were seeking answers to the very same questions modern people have and modern investigation stands on their shoulders, as Newton might say, and it is arrogant and hubristic to dismiss what they did and took time to write down so we would know.

## IF THE BIBLE GETS IT RIGHT, WHY ARE SO MANY CHURCH LEADERS AGAINST THE MARKET?

This is a question I need to address. The historical church has not been a bastion of market-oriented thinking although this story is much more complex than many realize, the Church has been far from monolithic on this issue and we must remember the church is godly oriented but ultimately a human institution run by imperfect people. But it is appropriate and proper to address some common criticisms frequently lodged at the market system by theologians and offer a response. It is not my intent to explore all of them in as much detail here but while we are on the topic some of the more important criticisms need to be addressed. I have categorized them into a few common groups for easier understanding.

### First Error: Social Justice Misapplied

The Bible is very clear and very strong about the requirement to defend the oppressed, downtrodden, outcast, and so forth. God makes it the Christian's responsibility to be His hands and deliver His compassion to those who desperately need it. Many well-meaning Christians who take this seriously also want to not just heal wounds but prevent them and see the market system as the cause of much social injustice. Some question the morality of a system that creates significant wealth and income inequalities and think the system is driven by and rewards greed. We live and operate in a fallen world of sinful men. Nothing in this world is perfect, but careful thinking, which I hope this book inspires, requires that we not just dispose of the system without close examination of the alternatives. The first question should be, is the system a failure or is it so imperfectly implemented that it is not really able to work as intended?

This book is making the case that the Bible supports a market-oriented economic arrangement. Some may disagree but then the question that must be answered is, will the alternative be implemented perfectly? It is possible to make things worse, much worse. The historical record of market economies, however imperfectly implemented, lifting people out of poverty is unmatched by any other system. Collectivist and command systems have no historical record that comes close to matching what market arrangements have done. Part of the reason for that is that collectivist arrangements, by replacing private goals with public ones, interfere and prevent people from using their God-given talents and skills to the best of their ability to serve others. Some would call this immoral but even if that is not the case such economic organizations have failed to create wealth and prosperity. Historical and modern cases abound. Properly applied social justice motivations would be to see the huge advantages of the market system in both morality of allowing people the freedom to pursue their own interests based on their own God-given skills and talents and the practical fact that markets are truly wealth creation machines which brings a number of other benefits such as better health, more opportunities, more resources to care for the marginalized, and for charity and social equity. The properly motivated and educated social justice warrior would seek to fix problems with the market system implementation, not scrap it for an alternative with no track record of success.

## Second Error: Equating Rich People to a System

Another common criticism is to see biblical critiques of wealth and the wealthy as a critique of the market system. Now this is interesting because it implies a tacit admission that the system that creates the most wealth is the market system. A person making this criticism has a hard time being consistent and also making the first criticism listed above. Few, if any, see a criticism of the wealthy as a criticism of any collectivist arrangement, in part that must be because it is assumed those systems do not create wealthy people. Of course, they do, but the wealth comes from exploitation and corruption, political connections and favors, not in serving others and creating value as in the market system. In a market system the wealthiest are business owners, in a collectivist system the wealthiest are politicians.

The criticisms of the wealthy in the Bible are almost exclusively aimed at wealth when used as a weapon or an idol. The wealthy criticized in the Old

Testament are abusive, lazy, and using their power and wealth to oppress. This is the exact opposite of how one gets wealthy in a market system which is by finding efficient ways to meet the needs of others. Wealth through oppression is the hallmark of cronyism and government gone wrong, where playing favorites and enriching some at the expense of others is the standard operating procedure, as God warned would happen through the prophet Samuel in 1 Samuel 8. It is a flaw in the system, not the system itself, and it is a flaw that does not disappear with different systems. So, a criticism of the wealthy in the Bible does not automatically equate with a criticism of a system, it is the criticism of a heart condition that wealth exposes and that is independent of any system other than the biological one.

## Third Error: Misunderstands the Market Process

Another criticism comes in the form of well-meaning theologians that do not have a firm understand of how the market process works. This is understandable, it is not their area of training, study, and expertise, but they should be humble enough to know the limits of their knowledge. For instance, Professor Craig Blomberg (see Appendix A for biography) writes that "neither system (markets or Socialism) necessarily helps the plight of the involuntarily poor, disabled, widow or orphan."[5] This shows a fundamental misreading of economic history. As discussed in the previous section, in no other system have the downtrodden and outcast had more mobility and opportunity and ultimately live better than in a market system, which again is why the social structure established in Deuteronomy is market oriented, God said take care of the widows, orphans, aliens, and poor and then gave a system that would effectively enable accomplishing that goal.

Market systems reward people who can serve and produce regardless of their situation. The 'rags to riches' stories are numerous and demonstrate where Blomberg may have misread economic history. Furthermore, the market system generates a tremendous amount of wealth that can be and is dedicated to caring for others who may not be economically productive or incapable of caring for themselves. Even the term *poor* is redefined in prosperous market economies. The median household income in the United States is approximately \$60,000[6] but to be in the infamous global upper 1 percent one needs to earn \$32,400.[7] The poverty line for a family of four in the United States is about \$25,000 and for a family of six it is \$34,590.[8] This means a family could be considered poor in the United States and in the global upper 1 percent simultaneously and even if not in the global 1 percent, one can be poor and relatively close to the global 1 percent (maybe the global 10–15 percent) if he lives in a country with a robust market economy. This is not to say there are not some truly poor people in market economies, there are and they need to be helped, but the first line of help for all poverty is God's way which is a market economy.

A second part of Blomberg's criticism (and I point to Blomberg not to criticize him in particular but because he is a very articulate presenter of this case) is that neither markets nor socialism adequately accounts for human depravity.[9] He is half right. Socialism assumes that each person has or can be forced to have a level of knowledge about and care for others the average person can only aspire to and thus it fails on its own internal expectations. For socialism to work the socialist planner needs to know quite a bit about what each person can do and needs and then be willing to put those needs into a proper hierarchy of the total social needs and then allocate resources to meet as many needs as possible. It is really an impossible task and for an interesting perspective the reader may like to view the charming and short very educational animated poem video by Russ Robert called *It's a Wonderful Loaf*.[10] Markets are quite different. Markets assume we are self-interested—some people equate this to greed and that is incorrect, but for the sake of argument we will consider them synonymous. Of course, greed is universal, all people have the impulse, some more than others and some act on it more than others, but it is not unique to an economic system, it is a human condition. But this is where we see the Miracle of the Market; it makes greedy, selfish, depraved people serve each other. This is an extremely important and often overlooked truth; markets are about cooperation and service. They take sinful, fallen, greedy, depraved people (and others who we may not describe quite so harshly) and aligns their incentives to cooperate with each other and to serve each other. Critics like to focus on the competition and how it may cause businesses to cheat and cut corners and so forth, that happens and those firms are usually punished when customers go elsewhere. But the prevailing operational mindset is one of cooperation; employer and employees have to cooperate, as do buyers and sellers, investors and entrepreneurs, and so on. There may disputes and issues, but in the end, people have to cooperate if anything is to get done and since all parties want to accomplish their goals, most cooperate with each other. Markets are a tool to create harmony, that *shalom* concept discussed earlier, where it would otherwise not exist. It is a system that accepts that humans are greedy and selfish and turns that impulse into service to others. The stereotype of Dickens's Scrooge makes for a great story but is completely wrong—greedy people cannot get wealthy in a market system by being mean and hard to be around, customers have choices and will not do business with such people. The only way Ebeneezer Scrooge, or any other evil movie business villain, got rich (short of being a crony or a crook) is by providing a good or a service to others at a price they are willing to pay. The market is a voluntary institution, people in it have to be wooed and persuaded and as long as they have choices, rude people exhibiting their greedy, selfish side will be at a disadvantage. And this is where the competition aspect comes in by creating benefits for good behavior and chasing the nasty and corrupt away.

Something frequently overlooked is that Karl Marx, the intellectual father and giant of collectivist thinking and policy, was no friend of Christianity. He saw it as a major problem and obstacle to his project of creating global Communism. He wanted religion in general eliminated and was particularly targeting Christianity which he saw as a tool of capitalist oppression. Christians who think that social justice lies in collectivist policies and such policies are biblically consistent would do well to remember Marx (and many others) disagreed. Marx, blinded by his own supposed brilliance, missed what was clearly in front of him. His system and its offshoots require a fundamental change in human nature that only Christianity actually prescribes for its adherents. Communism needs many conditions met to even work on paper but one important one is that it needs every member of society to care about others more then they care about themselves. That is contrary to human nature. Marx thought politics could change nature but experience shows us that is a failed hope, we know only Christ can change human nature, it is in Christian teaching not political theory, where people learn about loving your neighbor as yourself and the great love of sacrificing for others. This is a transformation politics has never been able to achieve and never can, hence the frustration of the practical communists and socialists; when people did not conform, we get the mass killings of over 100 million people that defined the twentieth century's experiments in applied collectivism. I cannot understand why anyone would ever want to experiment with this sort of system, it fails on all measures by its own standards and putting "Democratic" or "Christian" in front of "Socialism" does not make it work any better.

Marx misses the Miracle of the Market (and so much more). He misses that markets move people in the direction he claimed to want and desperately needed if his system had a prayer of working. Markets are about serving other people. A greedy, rapacious man behaves better in markets where voluntary cooperation is the driving force. Jeffrey Tucker captures this sentiment in his very insightful lecture called *Capitalism Is About Love*, in which he presents an apology of capitalism in an approach inspired by C.S. Lewis's *The Four Loves*. Tucker argues that liberty, religion, and property are inextricably bound together. Tucker explains how capitalism as defined by voluntary co-operation and private property creates a desire to trade and a level of affection between people as they seek to serve each other and make each other happy. He goes on to compare entrepreneurs to a romantic suitor who takes great risk and makes large sacrifices to woo customers but has no promise that the wooing will work since customers have other suitors.[11] In short, markets are about cooperation and service and turning man's fallen nature into beneficial outcomes and so many people miss that entirely.

## Fourth Error: The Definition of Charity

Adam Smith wrote his first book on moral sentiments and offered an explanatory reason for why people are sympathetic and engage in altruism. Of course, charity often begins with sympathetic feelings and sometimes that is enough. Stopping an inattentive person from walking into traffic can be motivated entirely by sympathy.

True charity requires action; Jesus said "*DO* unto others as you would have them *DO* unto you."[12] Charity means taking action and that requires resources. The market system is the system that has historically been the most successful in creating more resources which means it is the system that enables the most charity while requiring the least amount of it. Now many people recognize that resources are required to be charitable. But there is caveat, true charity means sacrifice, using one's own resources. It is impossible to be charitable with other people's resources, that is not charity. This means the charitable have to own things which means private property. And thus the irony is that the market social order is to be based on private property not only to create flourishing for the productive but also to enable the greatest amount of true charity. The collectivist impulse chokes production and turns charity into a farce of political redistribution which is often little more than vote buying in democratic systems.

## Fifth Error: Our Nature Is Fundamentally Different Than God's

While this is not the last of the errors people often make, it is the last one I want to discuss here and that is that many people make the error that human nature is fundamentally different from God's nature. Now, of course in one important sense it is, He is holy and perfect and we are fallen and sinful. But we are still created in His image and this is still His world and is (however imperfect) a reflection of His perfection. God uses market language and concepts throughout the entire Bible. He talks of giving a land the Israelites as their possession, we see language like paying the price of our sins and exchanging His righteousness for ours, the Latin phrase *O admirabile commercium* was often associated with Christmas in the Middle Ages. It translates, "O wonderful exchange" and is the source of the English word *commerce*, interesting that is was applied to the miracle of the Nativity.

If this is the language and the concepts God embraces, both in the prophetic era as well in the incarnation and church era (how many parables were economic in nature, even the Good Samaritan, the example many use for true charity was a merchant; he knew the road, knew the innkeeper and had a line of credit with him as well as extra cash on his person and traveled that way enough to be trusted, there is no other conclusion, he was a businessman) then why do we think that some other economic order is preferred and proper? It seems that the burden of proof is very high to prove that God intended us to operate in a system other than a market system. That fact alone exposes almost all collectivist schemes as being unbiblical. And, given that every system that has rejected and removed the institution of private property has descended into tyranny and oppression and failed to deliver better economic performance, that burden of proof has not been met in any measurable way.

## FINAL THOUGHTS

At this point, I need to come back to an opening statement, the Bible is a spiritual document and its main purpose is not economics. However, it has many secondary points and Christians need to understand what the Bible says and what that means for living life both personally and in larger society. The West is rich and many, dare I say most, do not really know why. They think it was luck. Or the West had and have more powerful guns, superior responses to germs, and made better steel. Or we exploited African slaves and near-slave Irish and Chinese. Or any number of other explanations, all of which range from woefully inadequate to completely wrong. There is not enough space here to address all of these but there are many sources available and I encourage the curious to look into them. The West is wealthy, in spite of its flaws and errors, because it largely followed the very path presented here. Not all at once and certainly not perfectly, but nonetheless it is the biblical foundation on which the West is built and ironically is now trying to tear down. As Rodney Stark wrote:

> During the past century, Western intellectuals have been more than willing to trace European imperialism to Christian origins, but they have been entirely unwilling to recognize that Christianity made any contribution (other than intolerance) to the Western capacity to dominate. Rather, the West is said to have surged ahead precisely as it overcame religious barriers to progress, especially those impeding science. The success of the West, including the rise of science, rested entirely on religious foundations and the people who brought it about were devout Christians.[13]

Sadly, not just most Americans but most Christians do not even realize this. We see this economic and theological ignorance on display in many ways. An unfortunate number (which means more than zero) of young Christians hold socialist economic views and think the Bible supports them, due to the overall dreadful job economists do in communicating the miracle of the market process to the people who need to hear it and due to a less than rigorous theological education young Christians are getting these days.

All of this would be bad enough if the West was only undermining its own system but its experts have exported these bad ideas to the developing world as well. Western advice and aid has disrupted markets, stymied growth, and enriched corrupt dictators in the developing world by advocating all sorts of policies for the developing world that the West itself never tried or implemented. The hubris of Western experts is on display thinking they discovered or can invent some other path to prosperity. It is either economic policy malpractice by the West or a complete intellectual break with its own history that the West would operate as though there is a different path to prosperity. Either way, the developing world is well served to ignore this advice, reject the aid model and the aid, and look at the history of the West. If one does that one will see that many of the policies reflect the points laid out in this book: a growing respect for human rights (slow but there), protection of property rights, an unbiased legal system, markets, trade, limited government that mostly knew its place, respect for innovation and the entrepreneur. Could the West have done better? Of course, just like Israel could have done better. The West's path to prosperity was very bumpy and had some significant lows but at the end of the day even with it under attack and largely misunderstood, it has created more wealth and prosperity and all that goes with it than any other system ever. Why? Because it is biblical and is God's order and his order works best.

## NOTES

1. For the alert or historically minded this was intentional. I converted Lenin's famous book title on how to build a Marxist revolution into a tool to study the market order, I thought it clever.

2. Manfred A. Max-Neef, *From the Outside Looking In: Experiences in "Barefoot Economics"* (London: Atlantic Highlands, New Jersey, USA : Zed Books, 1992). Max-Neef has recounted this story on numerous occasions and in several different venues but he shared it with me in July 2007 when I guest lectured at Universidad Austral.

3. *New Video of Jonathan Gruber Calling the American Peopole "Stupid" Has Surfaced*, n.d.

4. As a way of correcting Professor Gruber's characterization of the American people I offer this insight into the ACA, it was not his main point, which centered around tax incidence, but it is an important point. The legislation promised to cover more people *and* lower costs. How can it increase the number of customers (demand) and lower costs? When more people want something, including health care, the price of it increases unless supply (in this case medical professionals), increases even more. If the number of people wanting bread suddenly increased by 10 percent but the supply of bread was unchanged, prices would increase or there would be sellouts and empty shelves and some would go without, until prices increased. The trick in the bill is that it lowered prices for some, the old and sick, by forcing others, the young healthy people, to get insurance or pay a fine (tax). This was the heart of the Supreme Court case. Young healthy people do not use insurance so the money they pay into the system goes to help pay for the old and sick who are not being charged the full price for the services they use. The bill was little more than a transfer of wealth from the young and healthy to the old and sick, by the way, is also a transfer between a group that tends not to vote (young) and to a group that tends to vote in high numbers (old). But all of this lets the politicians claim the bill covers more people by forcing the young to get insured and brings costs down by subsidizing the old and sick—very clever, but it does not actually address any of the problems in the health care system.

5. Craig L. Blomberg, "Neither Capitalism nor Socialism: A Biblical Theology of Economics," *Journal of Markets and Morality* 15, no. 1 (Spring 2012): 212, https://www.marketsandmorality.com/index.php/mandm/article/viewFile/705/685.

6. "Median Household Income in the United States" (U.S. Bureau of the Census, September 12, 2018), https://fred.stlouisfed.org/series/MEHOINUSA646N.

7. Daniel Kurt, "Are You in the Top One Percent of the World?," *Investopedia*, February 8, 2019, https://www.investopedia.com/articles/personal-finance/050615/are-you-top-one-percent-world.asp.

8. "2018 Poverty Guidelines" (U.S. Department of Health and Human Services, February 7, 2018), https://aspe.hhs.gov/poverty-guidelines.

9. Blomberg, "Neither Capitalism nor Socialism: A Biblical Theology of Economics," 214.

10. *It's a Wonderful Loaf*, n.d., https://www.youtube.com/watch?v=ljULutAUL7o.

11. *Capitalism Is About Love* (Acton Institute, Grand Rapids, MI, 2015), https://www.youtube.com/watch?v=XUDHZ5sYOZg&t=1819s.

12. *Matthew*, n.d., 7:10 (ESV).

13. Rodney Stark, *The Victory of Reason: How Christianity Led to Freedom, Capitalism, and Western Success*, Random House trade pbk. ed (New York: Random House Trade Paperbacks, 2006), xi.

# Appendix A

## *Biographies*

A number of people are mentioned as influential thinkers and writers. Below is a brief biography of each.

### ADAM SMITH[1, 2]

Adam Smith (1723–1790) was a Scottish moral philosopher who is best known as the author of *An Inquiry into the Nature and Causes of the Wealth Of Nations* (1776), possibly one of the most influential books ever written. In this book Smith explained and explored the basis for a prosperous society as one that allows people to pursue their own goals and use their talents and abilities through specialization and the division of labor and achieve those goals through trade and commerce. He described this as self-interest, the idea that we know ourselves best and seek our own good and are best able to accomplish that but in so doing we serve others, and are led, as if by an invisible hand to provide benefits to others in the process of trying to provide benefits for ourselves. Smith also wrote an earlier book, *The Theory of Moral Sentiments* (1759), in which he explored charity and sympathy which was well received in its time. Smith saw his two works as complementary in an effort to explain human behavior and morality.

### DEIDRE MCCLOSKEY[3]

Deirdre N. McCloskey taught at the University of Illinois at Chicago from 2000 to 2015 as a distinguished professor of economics, history, English, and communication. She also spent twelve years (1968–1980) at the University of Chicago as a professor of economics and history. She is a Harvard graduate and has written seventeen books and close to four hundred scholarly articles. She describes herself as a Christian libertarian. Her works referenced in this book are the Bourgeois Trilogy, a sweeping treatise on why the modern approach to economics cannot really explain the modern world.

## RODNEY STARK[4]

Rodney Stark received his Ph.D. from the University of California, Berkeley, where he held appointments as a research sociologist at the Survey Research Center and at the Center for the Study of Law and Society. He left Berkeley to become professor of sociology and of comparative religion at the University of Washington. In 2004 he joined the faculty of Baylor University. He has published thirty-nine books and more than 150 scholarly articles. He is past president of the Society for the Scientific Study of Religion and of the Association for the Sociology of Religion.

## WILLIAM EASTERLY[5]

William Easterly is professor of economics at New York University and co-director of the NYU Development Research Institute. He is the author of three books and published more than sixty peer-reviewed academic articles, and has written columns and reviews for the *New York Times*, *Wall Street Journal*, *Financial Times*, *New York Review of Books*, and *Washington Post*. He has served as co-editor of the *Journal of Development Economics* and as director of the blog Aid Watch. He is a research associate of NBER, and senior fellow at BREAD.

## DAVID HUME[6]

David Hume (May 7, 1711–April 26, 1776) was a Scottish Enlightenment philosopher and scholar of many topics. He was a senior contemporary and friend of Adam Smith's. He is probably best known for his influential philosophical empiricism and naturalism. He was an atheist who argued against the existence of God and supposedly viewed his lack of progress in convincing others of this view as a major failure. That aside, Hume is considered one of, if not the, most important English-speaking philosopher but also wrote a definitive history of England, works on political theory, ethics, religion, and reason.

## HERMAN CHINERY-HESSE[7]

Chinery-Hesse is a technology entrepreneur in Ghana. With no start-up capital and little in the form of personal savings, no infrastructure, and no equipment other than his old personal computer, he started a software company in his bedroom of his parent's home. The company, called the SOFTtribe now employs around seventy people and has a client base of more than 250 organizations, including major multinationals such as the Ford Foundation, Nestlé, and Unilever; it is also a Microsoft development partner in the region. Herman is a manufacturing engineer by education but a software engineer by profession having graduated in industrial technology from Texas University, San Marcos. He holds a number of directorships and is an assessor of the Commercial Court, Ghana. He has also won a number of personal awards including being the only African recipient of the "Distinguished Alumnus Award" from the Texas State Alumni Association and Texas State University-San Marcos.

## DAMBISA MOYO[8]

Dambisa Moyo is a global economist and author who analyzes the macroeconomy and international affairs. She advises companies, corporate boards, CEOs, and management on investment decisions, capital allocation, and risk management. Her work examines the interplay of international business and the global economy, while highlighting key opportunities for investment; capitalizing on her rare ability to translate trends in markets, politics, regulatory matters, and economics into their likely impact on global business. She serves on the boards of Barclays Bank, the financial services group, and Chevron, the energy corporation. She previously served on the board of Barrick Gold, the global miner, SABMiller, the global brewer and Seagate Technology. Dambisa was named by *TIME* magazine as one of the "100 Most Influential People in the World," and was awarded the 2013 Hayek Lifetime Achievement Award.

## FRANCIS SCHAEFFER[9]

Francis August Schaeffer (January 30, 1912–May 15, 1984) was a Christian theologian, philosopher, and Presbyterian pastor. He was the author of twenty-two books and the founder of the L'abri Fellowship, a Christian study center based in Switzerland with satellite facilities in several nations. Schaeffer is known for his work in Christianity and culture and apologetics.

## MANFRED MAX-NEEF[10]

Manfred Max-Neef is a Chilean economist. He started his career as a professor of economics at the University of California, Berkeley in the early 1960s and is known for his taxonomy of human scale development. Max-Neef traveled through Latin America and the United States, as a visiting professor in various universities, as well as living with and researching the poor. He worked with the problem of development in the Third World, describing the inappropriateness of conventional models of development that have contributed to poverty, debt, and ecological disasters for Third World communities. In 1981, Max-Neef wrote *From the Outside Looking In: Experiences in Barefoot Economics*, a narrative of his travels among the poor in South America. In the same year, he founded the Centre for Development Alternatives (CEPAUR).

## CRAIG BLOMBERG[11]

Dr. Blomberg completed his PhD in New Testament, specializing in the parables and the writings of Luke–Acts, at Aberdeen University in Scotland. He received an MA from Trinity Evangelical Divinity School, and a BA from Augustana College. Before joining the faculty of Denver Seminary, he taught at Palm Beach Atlantic College and was a research fellow in Cambridge, England, with Tyndale House. In addition to writing numerous articles in professional journals, multi-author works, and dictionaries or encyclopedias, he has authored or edited twenty books.

## NOTES

1. "Adam Smith," in *The Library of Economics and Liberty* (Carmel, IN, USA: Liberty Fund, July 2018), https://www.econlib.org/library/Enc/bios/Smith.html.
2. Eamon Butler, "About Adam Smith," n.d., https://www.adamsmith.org/about-adam-smith.
3. Deirdre N. McCloskey, "Deidre N. McCloskey: Biography," n.d., http://www.deirdremccloskey.com/books/index.php.
4. "Rodney Stark: Biography," n.d., http://www.baylorisr.org/about-isr/distinguished-professors/rodney-stark/.
5. "William Easterly: Biography," n.d., http://www.williameasterly.org/.
6. James Fieser, "David Hume," in *Internest Encyclopedia of Philosophy*, n.d., https://www.iep.utm.edu/hume/.

7. "The Judges," *BBC Worldservice*, n.d., http://www.bbc.co.uk/worldservice/specials/1631_judges/page5.shtml.

8. "Dambisa Moyo: Biography," n.d., http://dambisamoyo.com/about/.

9. Udo Middlemann, "About The Francis A. Schaeffer Foundation," n.d., http://www.theschaefferfoundation.com/.

10. "Manfred Max-Neef," n.d., http://www.max-neef.cl/.

11. "Faculty Bios: Craig Blomberg," n.d., https://denverseminary.edu/about/faculty/member/86444/.

# Appendix B

## *Laws from the Ancient Near-East*

### THE CODE OF UR-NAMMU[1]

Ur-Nammu (reigned 2047–2030 BCE) was the founder of the Third Dynasty of Ur in Sumer who initiated the so-called Ur III Period (2047–1750 BCE) also known as the Sumerian Renaissance. He is best known as the king who composed the first complete law code in the world, the Code of Ur-Nammu. An earlier law code (known as the Code of Urukagina from the twenty-fourth century BCE) is only known through partial references to it and so, since the actual text itself has not been found, Ur-Nammu's code is considered the oldest extant.

The Code of Ur-Nammu assumed a universal understanding on the part of the people that law descended from the gods and the king was simply the administrator of those laws. Harsh penalties were considered unnecessary for the majority of crimes as, since people were assumed to know how they should behave toward each other, a monetary fine as a reminder of how to behave was sufficient. Kriwaczek writes:

> Although it is neither a true law code, being far from comprehensive; nor, some say, even introduced by Ur-Nammu but by his son Shulgi, code or no, although we only have fragments, they are enough to show that the laws covered both civil and criminal matters. Among criminal provisions it specifies which should be capital offences: murder, robbery, deflowering another man's virgin wife, and adultery when committed by a woman. For other misdemeanors the penalty was a fine in silver . . . [Ur-Nammu's code stands] in contrast to the more famous laws of Hammurabi, drafted some three centuries later, with its savage provisions of 'an eye for an eye, a tooth for a tooth' (148–149).

The Code is comprised of forty paragraphs that state the crime and the punishment that would be administered by the state through the will of the gods. Some examples of the laws are:

If a man committed a kidnapping, he is to be imprisoned and pay fifteen shekels of silver.
If a man proceeded by force, and deflowered the virgin slave-woman of another man, that man must pay five shekels of silver.
If a man appeared as a witness, and was shown to be a perjurer, he must pay fifteen shekels of silver.
If a man knocked out the eye of another man, he shall weigh out half a mina of silver.
If a man knocked out a tooth of another man, he shall pay two shekels of silver.
If a man, in the course of a scuffle, smashed the limb of another man with a club, he shall pay one mina of silver.

## CODE OF HAMMURABI[2]

Hammurabi was the first king of the Babylonian Empire, reigning from 1792 B.C.–1750 B.C. During his time in power, he conquered Sumer and Akkad, amassing those cultures for his territory. He is probably best known for his enduring code of Babylonian laws, known as Hammurabi's Code.

Hammurabi's code stands today as a fundamental example of laws that are so simple that they cannot be altered by anyone, not even a king. The laws, 282 of them in total, catalog a number of crimes and their applicable punishments, with little or no provision for the accused to offer explanation in his own defense.

## SOME OF THE LAWS ACCORDING TO HAMMURABI

If a man accuses another of a crime, but can't prove it, the accuser will be put to death. If a man accuses another of a crime, and can prove it, the accuser shall receive a monetary reward. If a robber is caught while stealing, he is to be put to death. If a man marries a woman, but has no relations with her, it is not considered a marriage. If a slave strikes his owner, his ear shall be cut off. If a son strikes his mother, his hands shall be cut off.

## THE TEN COMMANDMENTS[3]

"I am the Lord your God, who brought you out of the land of Egypt, out of the house of slavery.

"You shall have no other gods before me.

"You shall not make for yourself a carved image, or any likeness of anything that is in heaven above, or that is in the earth beneath, or that is in the water under the earth. You shall not bow down to them or serve them, for I the Lord your God am a jealous God, visiting the iniquity of the fathers on the children to the third and the fourth generation of those who hate me, but showing steadfast love to thousands of those who love me and keep my commandments.

"You shall not take the name of the Lord your God in vain, for the Lord will not hold him guiltless who takes his name in vain.

"Remember the Sabbath day, to keep it holy. Six days you shall labor, and do all your work, but the seventh day is a Sabbath to the Lord your God. On it you shall not do any work, you, or your son, or your daughter, your male servant, or your female servant, or your livestock, or the sojourner who is within your gates. For in six days the Lord made heaven and earth, the sea, and all that is in them, and rested on the seventh day. Therefore the Lord blessed the Sabbath day and made it holy.

"Honor your father and your mother, that your days may be long in the land that the Lord your God is giving you.

"You shall not murder.

"You shall not commit adultery.

"You shall not steal.

"You shall not bear false witness against your neighbor.

"You shall not covet your neighbor's house; you shall not covet your neighbor's wife, or his male servant, or his female servant, or his ox, or his donkey, or anything that is your neighbor's."

## NOTES

1. Joshua Mark, "Ur-Nammu," in *Ancient History Encyclopedia*, n.d., https://www.ancient.eu/Ur-Nammu/.
2. "Hammurabi's Code: Babylonian Law Set in Stone," n.d., https://www.ancient.eu/article/68/hammurabis-code-babylonian-law-set-in-stone/.
3. *Exodus*, n.d., 20:2–18 (ESV).

# Bibliography


"2018 Poverty Guidelines." U.S. Department of Health and Human Services, February 7, 2018. https://aspe.hhs.gov/poverty-guidelines.

"Adam Smith." In *The Library of Economics and Liberty*. Carmel, IN, USA: Liberty Fund, July 2018. https://www.econlib.org/library/Enc/bios/Smith.html.

Babatunde, Mark. "Africa's Highest Paid Members of Parliament." *Face2face Africa*, February 5, 2018.

Bastiat, Frederic. *The Law*. Dean Russell, Translator. Foundation for Economics Education: Irvington-on-the-Hudson. 1998.

Bauer, Peter, T. *Reality and Rhetoric*. Harvard University Press: Cambridge and London. 1984.

Bauer, Peter, T. *Dissent on Development*. Harvard University Press: Cambridge. 1971.

Blomberg, Craig L. "Neither Capitalism nor Socialism: A Biblical Theology of Economics." *Journal of Markets and Morality* 15, no. 1 (Spring 2012). https://www.marketsandmorality.com/index.php/mandm/article/viewFile/705/685.

Bradley, Anne and Art Lindsley. ed. *For the Least of These: A Biblical Answer to Poverty*. Westbow Press: Bloomington, IN. 2014.

Bradley, Anne and Art Lindsley. ed. *Counting the Cost: Christian Perspectives on Capitalism*. Abilene Christian University Press: Abilene, TX. 2017

Butler, Eamon. "About Adam Smith," n.d. https://www.adamsmith.org/about-adam-smith.

*Capitalism Is About Love*. Acton Institute, Grand Rapids, MI, 2015. https://www.youtube.com/watch?v=XUDHZ5sYOZg&t=1819s.

Central Intelligence Agency. *The World Factbook*, n.d. https://www.cia.gov/library/publications/the-world-factbook/geos/sn.html.

"Dambisa Moyo: Biography," n.d. http://dambisamoyo.com/about/.

Easterly, William. *The Elusive Quest for Growth*. The MIT Press: Cambridge and London. 2002.

"Faculty Bios: Craig Blomberg," n.d. https://denverseminary.edu/about/faculty/member/86444/.

Fieser, James. "David Hume." In *Internet Encyclopedia of Philosophy*, n.d. https://www.iep.utm.edu/hume/.

Fukuyama, Francis. *Trust: The Social Virtues and the Creation of Prosperity*. New York: Free Press, 1995.

"GDP Per Capita, PPP (Currrent International $)." The World Bank, n.d. https://data.worldbank.org/indicator/NY.GDP.PCAP.PP.CD?view=chart,.

Grudem, Wayne and Barry Asmus. *The Poverty of Nations*. Crossway: Wheaton, IL. 2013.

Hayek, F.A. *The Constitution of Liberty.* Chicago: University of Chicago Press. Reprint. Chicago: Henry Regnery, 1972.

Hill, Andrew, and John Walton. *A Survey of the Old Testament*. Grand Rapids, MI: Zondervan Publishing House, 1991.

Holy Bible: English Standard Version, Crossway Bibles, Wheaton, IL. 2001.

"Human Rights Risk Index 2016–Q4." Verisk Maplecroft, December 8, 2016. https://reliefweb.int/sites/reliefweb.int/files/resources/2016_ITF_Human_Rights_Index_2016–01.pdf.

*It's a Wonderful Loaf*, n.d. https://www.youtube.com/watch?v=ljULutAUL7o.

Kirzner, Israel M. *Competition and Entrepreneurship*. 7. Dr. Chicago: Univ. of Chicago Press, 1993.

Kline, Meredith G. *Treaty of the Great King: The Covenant Structure of Deuteronomy*. Eugene, OR: Wipf & Stock Publishers, 1963.

Kurt, Daniel. "Are You in the Top One Percent of the World?" *Investopedia*, February 8, 2019. https://www.investopedia.com/articles/personal-finance/050615/are-you-top-one-percent-world.asp.

Landes, David. *The Wealth and Poverty of Nations: Why Some are So Rich and Some So Poor*. W.W. Norton& Co.: New York and London. 1999.

"Manfred Max-Neef," n.d. http://www.max-neef.cl/.

Max-Neef, Manfred A. *From the Outside Looking In: Experiences in "Barefoot Economics."* London: Atlantic Highlands, New Jersey, USA : Zed Books, 1992.

McCloskey, Deidre N. *The Bourgeois Virtues: Ethics for an Age of Commerce*. The University of Chicago Press: Chicago. 2006.

McCloskey, Deidre N. *Bourgeois Dignity: Why Economics Can't Explain the Modern World*. The University of Chicago Press: Chicago. 2010.

McCloskey, Deidre N. *Bourgeois Equality: How Ideas, Not Capital or Institutions Enriched the World. Why Economics Can't Explain the Modern World*. The University of Chicago. Press: Chicago. 2016.

McCloskey, Deirdre N. "Deidre N. McCloskey: Biography," n.d. http://www.deirdremccloskey.com/books/index.php.

"Median Household Income in the United States." U.S. Bureau of the Census, September 12, 2018. https://fred.stlouisfed.org/series/MEHOINUSA646N.

Merelli, Annalisa. "In Italy, Members of Parliament Make Five Times More than the Average Worker." *Quartz Ideas*. March 4, 2014. https://qz.com/183305/in-italy-members-of-parliament-make-five-times-more-than-the-average-worker/.

Middlemann, Udo. "About The Francis A. Schaeffer Foundation," n.d. http://www.theschaefferfoundation.com/.

Miller, Michael, M. *Poverty Cure.* Acton Media: Grand Rapids, MI. 2012.

*New Video of Jonathan Gruber Calling the American Peopole "Stupid" Has Surfaced*, n.d.

Peterson, Jordan B. *12 Rules for Life: An Antidote to Chaos*. London: Allen Lane, 2018.

"Rodney Stark: Biography," n.d. http://www.baylorisr.org/about-isr/distinguished-professors/rodney-stark/.

Roser, Max, and Esteban Ortiz-Ospina. "Global Extreme Poverty," March 2017. https://ourworldindata.org/extreme-poverty.

Smith, Adam. *An Inquiry in the Nature and Causes of the Wealth of Nations.* Edwin Cannan, editor. Methuen and Co.: London. 1904.

Stark, Rodney. *The Victory of Reason: How Christianity Led to Freedom, Capitalism, and Western Success*. Random House trade pbk. ed. New York: Random House Trade Paperbacks, 2006.

*The CIA World Factbook*. Washington, D.C.: United States Government, n.d. https://www.cia.gov/library/publications/the-world-factbook/wfbExt/region_afr.html.

"The Judges." *BBC Worldservice*, n.d. http://www.bbc.co.uk/worldservice/specials/1631_judges/page5.shtml.

"Time Required to Start a Business (Days)." The World Bank, n.d. https://data.worldbank.org/indicator/IC.REG.DURS?view=chart.

UNESCO Institute for Statistics. "Literacy Rate, Youth Female (% of Females Ages 15–24)." The World Bank, n.d. https://data.worldbank.org/.

"Why Japanese Houses Have Such Limited Lifespans." *The Economist*, March 15, 2018. https://www.economist.com/finance-and-economics/2018/03/15/why-japanese-houses-have-such-limited-lifespans.

"William Easterly: Biography," n.d. http://www.williameasterly.org/.

# Index

# About the Author

**Brian Baugus** is assistant professor of economics at Regent University in Virginia Beach, Virginia. He holds a Ph.D. and MA in economics from George Mason University, an MBA from Vanderbilt University, and a BA in economics from McDaniel College. This is his first book but he has published several articles in both the popular and academic press. He, along with his co-author, was the 2016–17 Michael Szenberg Prize winner for most original article published by the *American Economist* in those years. He has lectured on the biblical basis of free market economics at a number of conferences in sub-Sahara Africa and has an ongoing teaching and consulting relationship with entrepreneurs and think-tank leaders in several nations. He is married and lives with his wife, three of their children (the oldest has moved on her own), and assorted pets in the Tidewater/Hampton Roads area of Virginia.

www.ingramcontent.com/pod-product-compliance
Lightning Source LLC
Chambersburg PA
CBHW051252200926
51612CB00001B/15
* 9 7 8 1 4 9 8 5 6 9 8 1 1 *